THE FUTURE OF U.S.-TAIWAN RELATIONS

HEARING

BEFORE THE

SUBCOMMITTEE ON ASIA AND THE PACIFIC

OF THE

COMMITTEE ON FOREIGN AFFAIRS
HOUSE OF REPRESENTATIVES

ONE HUNDRED FOURTEENTH CONGRESS

SECOND SESSION

FEBRUARY 11, 2016

Serial No. 114–153

Printed for the use of the Committee on Foreign Affairs

Available via the World Wide Web: http://www.foreignaffairs.house.gov/ or
http://www.gpo.gov/fdsys/

U.S. GOVERNMENT PUBLISHING OFFICE

98–605PDF   WASHINGTON : 2016

For sale by the Superintendent of Documents, U.S. Government Publishing Office
Internet: bookstore.gpo.gov   Phone: toll free (866) 512–1800; DC area (202) 512–1800
Fax: (202) 512–2104   Mail: Stop IDCC, Washington, DC 20402–0001

CONTENTS

THE FUTURE OF U.S.–TAIWAN RELATIONS

THURSDAY, FEBRUARY 11, 2016

House of Representatives,
Subcommittee on Asia and the Pacific,
Committee on Foreign Affairs,
Washington, DC.

The subcommittee met, pursuant to notice, at 2 o'clock p.m., in room 2200 Rayburn House Office Building, Hon. Matt Salmon (chairman of the subcommittee) presiding.

Mr. Salmon. Subcommittee will come to order.

First of all and foremost, my heart goes out to Taiwan as it deals with the aftermath of the shocking magnitude 6.4 earthquake on February 6th that claimed 63 lives and injured 551, and that was in the city of Tainan, where I lived for 7 months, and I have a really special place in my heart for the people of Tainan.

I am so saddened to hear about the damage that the earthquake wreaked and I know I am joined with my colleagues of the subcommittee in continuing to support Taiwan in this difficult time.

Today, we celebrate Taiwan's democracy, given its recent Presidential and parliamentary elections in January. In this regional context, Taiwan's free and fair elections, vibrant free market economy and open society have definitely set an example for the region and for the world.

With the Democratic Progressive Party, DPP, victory, the party has won its first ever absolute majority in the Legislative Yuan which until—which has until now been controlled by the Kuomintang, KMT. President-elect Tsai Ing-wen will also be Taiwan's first female President and I think that is pretty exciting.

This third peaceful transfer of executive power is an indication of the maturation of Taiwan's democracy. The recent election presents the United States with more opportunities to improve our political security and economic relationship with Taiwan.

We are here to parse out the priorities of President-elects Tsai's administration and understand the prospects and potential for the U.S., Taiwan and the cross-Strait relationships and to discuss how the United States can continue to honor our commitments to Taiwan. I look forward to hearing from our distinguished witnesses on these important issues.

The cross-Strait relationship has been relatively stable under the sitting Kuomintang President Ma Ying-jeou. President Ma took strides to build closer relationships with China, especially in trade.

To his credit, President Ma negotiated the Economic Cooperation Framework Agreement, ECFA, with China in 2010 and this paved the way for Taiwan's expanded trade ties under similar economic cooperation agreements with New Zealand and Singapore.

The suspension on the cross-Strait Trade in Services Agreement, TISA, as a result of domestic protests in 2014 may have indirectly contributed to China's tightening on further trade agreements between Taiwan and other countries.

With slow economic development, untapped potential due to political constraints and heavy reliance on trade, I look forward to hearing from our distinguished panels, especially our administration witness, about Taiwan's economic and trade prospects and how the United States can help Taiwan overcome some of these challenges.

I also worry about the potential for cross-Strait stability as China has not hesitated to remind us that it is still willing to use military force against Taiwan.

Of note, China continues to press President-elect Tsai and her administration to acknowledge the 1992 consensus, something President Ma has adhered to.

President-elect Tsai will continue to face pressure here, given her party's own interpretation of the agreement. Despite underscoring her intention to maintain the status quo and saying there won't be provocation and there won't be surprises, we cannot say the same for China.

A steady stream of threats toward Taiwan's national security are an everyday reality for Taiwan and its people and I hope our panelists can shed light on how we can continue to support Taiwan's security under the Taiwan Relations Act and through increased cooperation.

I admire outgoing President Ma and all that he was able to accomplish for Taiwan. I look forward to seeing how we can continue to work with President Tsai for the mutual benefit of the United States and Taiwan.

Members of Congress have always shared a strong interest in supporting Taiwan's security and democracy. Having lived there for a few years myself while serving a church mission, I am one of its big supporters—hopefully, its biggest.

At a time when Taiwan's presence in the international arena is constantly being threatened, at a time when Taiwan's security is not insured from coercion and potential attacks, I urge our administration to continue to support Taiwan.

We must prioritize Taiwan's active and meaningful participation on the global stage, ensure its self-defense capabilities are sufficient and ensure that its economy continues to grow vibrantly and compete with other major powers in the region.

Members present today are going to be permitted to submit written statements to be included in the official hearing record.

Without objection, the hearing record will remain open for 5 calendar days to allow for statements, questions and extraneous material subject to the length limitation in the rules.

And I am going to recognize Chairman Royce and then Ranking Member Sherman.

Mr. ROYCE. Thank you very much, Chairman Salmon.

And let me first say on behalf of our members here we have all visited Tainan and been in Taiwan and our hearts go out to the people of Taiwan, to the victims of this earthquake. Fifty-nine perished so far. Hundreds and hundreds have been injured. There is a great knowledge here in the United States in terms of how much the Taiwanese go to the rescue with volunteers all over the world after international incidents whenever an earthquake or some other disaster hits. We saw how quickly the authorities, but also how quickly the volunteers, rushed to the scene to begin to rescue people.

So we have traveled—our committee together since I have been chairman—has traveled three times down to Taiwan in the last 3 years. We visited Kaohsiung and we have visited Tainan, as I mentioned, and Taipei, of course, and we are just devastated to see the destruction. But the American people stand by the Taiwanese people in their time of need and we are ready to assist in any way we can.

Taiwan is one of our most important friends to the U.S. in the Asia Pacific and I know that supporting Taiwan is a critical issue for members of the Foreign Affairs Committee. As chairman, I have made the strengthening of this relationship with Taiwan one of the committee's top priorities.

I want to again congratulate the people of Taiwan for their free and fair elections last month. I think the U.S. and Taiwan share a very important commitment to democracy, to human rights, to the rule of law and these values, I think, serve as a bedrock to the U.S.-Taiwan relationship. And I think the election demonstrated the strength and vibrancy of Taiwan's democracy and their democratic system, hopefully serving as a model for other countries in the region.

Last year, Chairman Salmon joined me, as I said, in the delegation where we spent some time in Taipei working to strengthen the U.S.-Taiwan relationship. We met with the sitting President, Ma. We met with President-elect, Dr. Tsai Ing-wen, and as the Taiwan Government changes hands during its transition period it is important that the U.S. continues to emphasize its steadfast commitment to Taiwan and that the players in Taiwan also make responsible decisions that are in the best interest of the people of Taiwan.

A stable and prosperous Taiwan is, of course, in the best interests of the United States and that is why I look forward to working closely with President-elect Tsai's new government to strengthen all aspects of the U.S.-Taiwan bilateral relationship. And in particular I have a enthusiasm—I have long been an advocate for Taiwan's inclusion into the Trans-Pacific Partnership. Taiwan's economic security is just as important as its physical security, so its inclusion in the second round of the agreement will be critical to Taiwan's stability. I know that Dr. Tsai will be willing to do the work in Taiwan needed to seriously begin a bilateral investment agreement with the United States with an eye toward TPP and so I encourage the administration to work with the new government to create a pathway for Taiwan to be integrated into these trade deals.

I am also committed to upholding the letter and spirit of the Taiwan Relations Act, which has underpinned the relationship now for 37 years.

Last year, we worked tirelessly to pressure the administration to finally follow through with the arms sales that it had promised Taiwan. The sales were finally set in motion in December but I remain deeply skeptical about the administration's delays that needlessly drag out the arms sales process for Taiwan.

So over the next year both the U.S. and Taiwan will be working on these types of issues, and I thank Chairman Salmon again—he is among the strongest friends of the Taiwanese people—and I also thank Congressman Brad Sherman and the other members of this committee for their engagement on the issue of Taiwan.

I look forward to hearing from the witnesses.

Mr. SALMON. Thank you.

The chair recognizes the ranking member, Mr. Sherman.

Mr. SHERMAN. Chairman, thank you for holding these hearings. I know we have a classified briefing for the full committee on the same subject as these hearings and then I know that we have votes.

So we will have a limited amount of time here in this room. Our hearts go out to the people of Taiwan and I join with your statement, the statement of our full committee chair, in sympathy for the people of Taiwan where this disaster has cost 60 lives.

And as the chairman noted, the people of Taiwan are there again and again and again when there is a disaster elsewhere in the world.

While the regime in Beijing is currently engaged in a concerted effort to restrict human rights, we look only at Taiwan as a country where democracy flourishes, and we will once again see the peaceful and democratic transfer of power from one party to another.

The United States has a strong interest in supporting the people of Taiwan and those interests are enshrined in the Taiwan Relations Act, which is an important statement that the U.S. to resolve that the people of Taiwan will be able to determine their own fate permanently and peacefully.

The clear message should be that the United States believes in the power of dialogue and we unequivocally support the right of the people of Taiwan to determine their own fate.

In that spirit, Mr. Chairman, I thank you for bringing up the Taiwan Naval Support Act and I thank the administration for finally delivering the frigging frigates.

While our commitment to our friends in Taiwan should not be doubted, I was very impressed to meet Dr. Tsai when she was in opposition on the trip led by Chairman Royce and I am confident that the people of Taiwan will rejoice when they inaugurate their first woman President and it is a joy that I look forward to the American people experiencing just a year later.

And I know the people of Taiwan will enjoy living under a woman President and I know my constituents look forward to that joy as well.

I look forward to hearing how we can help diversify the economy of Taiwan so it is less reliant on and dependent on and subject to manipulation by the People's Republic of China.

I support Taiwan joining TPP if that is what the people of China want—the people of Taiwan want. What I don't support is the United States joining TPP, and I will point out that every candidate for President that is able to get more than 3 percent of the vote has taken a stance against TPP because they know that the American people wouldn't dream of seriously considering a candidate that supported this trade pact which will hurt the American people so significantly while helping the People's Republic of China establish that the rules of trade for the world are that currency manipulation is, as my people say, kosher.

It is a tremendous negotiating victory for the People's Republic of China to enshrine in the rules of the road that their practices of currency manipulation are to be sacrosanct, not to mention the fact that the rules of origin are of such tremendous assistance to the People's Republic of China.

Taiwan could play a useful and larger role in international organizations, sharing its expertise, sharing its experience.

The United States needs to continue to advocate broader participation for in Taiwan international organizations, whether it be those organizations like Interpol, that keep us safe from dangerous criminals, and that's why I have cosponsored legislation to direct the President to develop a strategy to obtain observer status at least for Taiwan and Interpol.

Similarly, I have advocated Taiwan's participation in other international organizations. There is no reason why the fine points of international sovereignty should get involved in the practicality of Taiwan's membership in WHO.

Even the People's Republic of China has it in their interest to stop criminals and stop disease and the practical way to do that is to involve Taiwan to the maximum extent in the international organizations that are focused on human health and international crime.

So I look forward to hearing from the witnesses here in this open setting and to then adjourning for the classified briefing.

And I don't know if anyone else on our side has an opening statement. But I hope the chairman would indulge at least one member on our side.

Mr. SALMON. Sure. I think Mr. Chabot has an opening statement.

Mr. CHABOT. Thank you, Mr. Chairman, and thank you for holding this important hearing. Considering the recent elections in Taiwan, I want to commend the subcommittee for calling this hearing.

I met with President-elect Tsai several times in the past, both here and in Taiwan, and I congratulate her and the people of Taiwan for their continued support of democracy.

And I want to say that I agree with my colleague, Mr. Sherman, which sometimes we agree and sometimes we don't, but I certainly agree with his sentiment about how wonderful it is that Taiwan has its first woman President.

As far as here in the U.S., I also share the sentiment of having the first woman President sworn in next year except that unfortunately——

Mr. CONNOLLY. Here in the United States?

Mr. CHABOT [continuing]. Because of New Hampshire Tuesday evening Carly Fiorina already dropped out. But in any event——

Mr. SHERMAN. Hence, there is only one way to achieve the goal that you and I both have for the United States.

Mr. CHABOT. And we may both have them this year. You never know.

Mr. CONNOLLY. Gee, Mr. Chairman, I was just about to give Mr. Chabot a big hug.

Mr. CHABOT. There you go.

Mr. SALMON. Yeah. He was talking about a brokered convention. I'm sorry.

Mr. CHABOT. But getting back to Taiwan, I would like to quickly address the restrictions on high-level visits by high-ranking Taiwanese officials, something that I have always felt was both insulting and counterproductive.

Years ago, I joined a number of my colleagues and we flew to New York City one evening to meet—after votes here to meet with then President Chen, who is a great friend of America.

We had to travel to New York because President Chen was not allowed to enter Washington, DC. This is U.S. policy, our own self-imposed restrictions, and I have long said that this policy is nonsense and should be changed.

In fact, then Foreign Minister Mark Chen when he was in the legislature I had met with him in Washington. He was appointed foreign minister and a few weeks later when we were going to get together I had to drive to Baltimore to meet with him there because he wasn't allowed—since he was one of the four top officials wasn't allowed to meet here in Washington, DC. That is outrageous. It is an insult to Taiwan and the United States should change this immediately.

I also urge the administration to have direct dialogue with the democratically-elected President of Taiwan and, as you all know, international diplomacy face-to-face meetings are an important component in ensuring a sustainable relationship.

And finally, I would like to note that I introduced H. Con. Res. 88 last fall. This legislation reaffirms that Taiwan Relations Act and the six assurances together form the cornerstone of U.S. relations with Taiwan. I would urge my colleagues to join in that support.

I yield back. Thank you, Mr. Chairman.

Mr. SALMON. Thank you. Mr. Connolly.

Mr. CONNOLLY. Thank you, Mr. Chairman.

Just real briefly, as a member of the committee and subcommittee and also as the co-chair of the Taiwan caucus, this is a very important hearing and events in the Strait are also very important.

We all can celebrate free and democratic elections that led to the change in government from one party to another and with the first female President of Taiwan, both welcome developments, and to watch the free transfer of power is a very powerful model in the region, one we hope will evolve and be replicated.

I agree with Mr. Chabot that the cornerstone of our relationship is the Taiwan Relations Act and the six assurances and that act includes interalia, a defensive military support posture on the part of the United States, to ensure that peace prevails in the Taiwan Straits and that whatever the evolution politically it will be a peaceful one, not any other kind of kinetic option.

So these are important hearings. Lots of changes going on including, tragically, the earthquake in Tainan and the loss of life there, and I am happy to be here and joining in these hearings.

And I thank you, Mr. Chairman, and our ranking member, Mr. Sherman, for holding them.

Mr. SALMON. Thank you.

Ms. Meng.

Ms. MENG. Thank you, Chairman Salmon, to our Ranking Member Sherman and all our distinguished witnesses who are here today. Thank you for attending this important hearing.

Before I go forward with my remarks, I also want to take a moment to acknowledge the earthquake in Taiwan this past Saturday.

It was a terrible tragedy and I know people, not just in Taiwan and around the world, but my constituents in New York are very concerned as well.

I know that rescue efforts are ongoing and I too want to thank all the volunteers and people who have come forward to help.

Both my colleagues and I will be keeping a close eye on the progress.

The purpose of today's hearing is to assess the future of U.S.-Taiwan relations, particularly in light of the January 16th Presidential elections, and I too want to extend my congratulations to Dr. Tsai as the first female President in Taiwan.

I congratulate the people of Taiwan for their steadfast adherence to democracy and I look forward to improving our robust relationship.

Thank you, and I yield back.

Mr. SALMON. Mr. Bera, if you would like to make a quick opening statement. You good?

Mr. Lowenthal, did you want to make a quick statement?

Mr. LOWENTHAL. I concur. First, I thank you for being here. You know, and I also want to extend my condolences to the families of all those that were killed and injured by the earthquake. I want to congratulate the people of Taiwan on the successful elections.

It is a welcome example of democracy in a region that at the same time has seen a great backsliding on human rights. That is not true in terms of Taiwan.

We have seen the gradual improvement in the relationships between the cross-Strait relations.

I think it is beneficial for the security of all to have that stability and I look forward to the hearing today. Thank you, and I yield back.

Mr. SALMON. Thank you very much.

We are going to go ahead and introduce our first panelist. Thank you so much for being here today, Ms. Thornton.

We are pleased to have Ms. Susan Thornton here today, deputy assistant secretary of state in the State Department's Bureau of East Asian and Pacific Affairs. And we would like to have you give your opening statement and have some questions and then we will excuse you and we will seat the next panel.

You understand the lighting system. Not real complicated. When it goes amber you got a minute and when it goes red, most of the time people keep talking around here, but you should stop.

Thank you. Ms. Thornton.

STATEMENT OF MS. SUSAN A. THORNTON, DEPUTY ASSISTANT SECRETARY, BUREAU OF EAST ASIAN AND PACIFIC AFFAIRS, U.S. DEPARTMENT OF STATE

Ms. THORNTON. Thank you very much, Mr. Chairman, members of the subcommittee for having me here today and giving me the opportunity to discuss our very strong relationship with Taiwan.

The story of Taiwan is, of course, an impressive one. People on Taiwan have built a prosperous, free and orderly society with strong institutions worthy of emulation and envy.

And before I go any further, I would also like to offer my sincere condolences to everyone in Taiwan that was affected by the recent earthquake, especially the families of those who were injured or lost their lives. The American people stand with the people on Taiwan during this difficult time.

Last month's free and fair elections were yet another victory for Taiwan's vibrant democracy. These elections not only represent Taiwan's third peaceful transition of Presidential power and the first transfer of power in its legislature but, as has been already remarked, will also lead to the inauguration of Taiwan's first female President.

In this administration we have worked to strengthen and deepen the bonds between the people of the United States and Taiwan to build a comprehensive, durable and mutually beneficial partnership.

As one of Taiwan's strongest partners, we are working side by side to increase our mutual economic prosperity, tackle global challenges and ensure effective security to support continued stability and dynamism for Taiwan and the region.

On trade issues, Taiwan has developed a well-earned reputation for having a diversified economy that has built its prosperity on the openness of the global trade system.

Taiwan has grown to become our ninth largest trading partner and our seventh largest destination for agricultural exports.

In 2015, our two-way trade in goods with Taiwan reached $66 billion, up 4½ percent in just the last 2 years. The United States has also moved up to be Taiwan's second largest trading partner in the last year.

Aside from these big business links, people-to-people ties between the United States and Taiwan also continue to grow. Travel for business and pleasure from Taiwan to the United States jumped 35 percent in 2013 alone after Taiwan became a member of the U.S. visa waiver program in November 2012.

The United States remains committed to supporting Taiwan's confidence and dignity through increased participation in the international community and enhanced security.

We continue to support Taiwan's membership in organizations that do not require statehood and to urge meaningful participation in those that do.

At a time when pressure to squeeze Taiwan out of international organizations is growing, we are finding new ways for Taiwan to earn the dignity and respect that its contributions to global challenges merit.

These include new innovations such as the establishment of our Global Cooperation and Training Framework. The GCTF is a vehicle for the United States to help showcase Taiwan's strengths and expertise by making it a hub for helping other countries to address global and regional concerns.

At the same time, we remain just as committed to Taiwan's meaningful participation in organizations like Interpol, ICAO, WHO and the U.N. climate framework.

We will continue to match Taiwan's growing capacity to serve the international community with equally innovative approaches to enabling and highlighting Taiwan's contributions.

On the security front, the United States makes available to Taiwan defense articles and services necessary for Taiwan to maintain a sufficient self-defense which is consistent with our responsibilities under the Taiwan Relations Act.

During the Obama administration, we have notified Congress of over $14 billion in arms sales to Taiwan including a sale of $1.83 billion that was notified in December of last year.

Our efforts at supporting Taiwan's self-defense capabilities extend beyond arms sales, however. We also support Taiwan's capacity-building efforts through visits, maintenance programs, and exchanges.

Due in part to these stepped-up contacts and strong U.S. partnership, Taipei has gained more confidence in its engagements with Beijing.

In recent years, the two sides have pursued constructive dialogue to reach agreements on economic and people-to-people exchanges that promote peace and stability across the Taiwan Strait.

Last year in November, we welcomed the meeting between leaders on both sides of the Taiwan Strait and the historic improvement in cross-Strait relations that it symbolized.

The United States remains committed to our one-China policy based on the three joint communiques and the Taiwan Relations Act, a policy that has remained consistent over several decades and many administrations.

We will continue to call on both sides of the Strait to engage in dialogue on the basis of dignity and respect after Taiwan's new administration takes office in May.

In conclusion, we have developed a vital partnership with Taiwan that is filled with many opportunities for cooperation in the future.

We are committed to ensuring that this relationship will continue to thrive as we find new ways to deepen our unofficial ties.

The innovative spirit, democratic dynamism and courageous vision of the people on Taiwan make us proud to be their friend and partner.

Mr. Chairman and members of the subcommittee, I would like to thank you again for inviting me here today and I'm happy to answer any questions you may have.

[The prepared statement of Ms. Thornton follows:]

Testimony of Susan Thornton
Deputy Assistant Secretary of State
Bureau of East Asian and Pacific Affairs, Department of State

House Foreign Affairs Committee
Subcommittee on Asia and the Pacific

February 11, 2016

Thank you Mr. Chairman and members of the Subcommittee for giving me the opportunity today to discuss our strong unofficial relationship with Taiwan.

The story of Taiwan is, of course, an impressive one. The people on Taiwan have built a prosperous, free, and orderly society with strong institutions, worthy of emulation and envy. Before I go any further, I would like to offer my sincere condolences to everyone in Taiwan that was affected by the recent earthquake, especially the families of those who lost their lives or were injured. The American people stand with the people on Taiwan during this difficult time.

Last month's free and fair elections were yet another victory for Taiwan's vibrant democracy. These elections not only represent Taiwan's third peaceful transition of presidential power and the first transfer of power in its legislature, but will also lead to the inauguration of Taiwan's first female president.

In this Administration, we have worked to strengthen and deepen the bonds between the people of the United States and Taiwan and to build a comprehensive, durable, and mutually beneficial partnership. As one of Taiwan's strongest partners, we are working side-by-side to increase our mutual economic prosperity, tackle global challenges, and ensure effective security to support continued stability and dynamism for Taiwan and the region.

On trade issues, Taiwan has developed a well-earned reputation for having a diversified economy that has built its prosperity on the openness of the global trade system. Just seven years ago, this island of 23 million people was our 15th largest export partner. Now, Taiwan has grown to become our **ninth**-largest overall trading partner and our **seventh**-largest destination for agricultural exports. In 2015, our two-way trade in goods with Taiwan exceeded $66 billion, which is a 4.5 percent increase from 2013. The United States has also moved up to be Taiwan's **second**-largest trading partner in the last year.

At the same time, Taiwan has also expressed an interest in further deepening its integration into the regional economy through trade and investment. We have been working closely through the U.S.-Taiwan Trade and Investment Framework Agreement (TIFA) talks to accelerate Taiwan's economic reform efforts, resolve longstanding trade issues, and press Taiwan to implement food safety regulations based on science and consistent with international standards. At the recent TIFA talks in October 2015, we discussed a broad range of issues including Taiwan's investment climate, intellectual property, medical devices and pharmaceuticals, and agricultural issues.

Our close trade links also reflect a growing investment relationship. In 2014, investment from Taiwan ranked 29th in total stock of foreign direct investment (FDI) with $9.9 billion. According to data from the Bureau of Economic Analysis, as of 2013, companies from Taiwan employed more than 12,000 workers in the United States with total worker compensation of almost a billion dollars. Moreover, Taiwan has repeatedly sent one of the largest delegations to our SelectUSA Investment Summit, showing continued active interest in the U.S. market. This investment relationship continues to produce more profitable opportunities for Taiwan businesses which, in turn, have created good-paying jobs for American workers.

Aside from these business links, people-to-people ties between the United States and Taiwan continue to grow. Travel for business and pleasure from Taiwan to the United States jumped 35 percent in 2013 alone, after Taiwan became a member of the U.S. Visa Waiver Program in November 2012. We expect these numbers to expand further as the U.S. and Taiwan finalize an agreement to facilitate more business travel through a trusted traveler program.

And let's not forget about the tens of thousands of students that Taiwan sends to the United States to receive a high-quality education. Last year, Taiwan was our **seventh** largest source of international students, higher than Japan, the UK, or Germany. In 2014, students from Taiwan contributed almost a billion dollars to the U.S. economy.

Even outside of the traditional classroom, through the Fulbright Program and the International Visitor Leadership Program (IVLP), young professionals and rising scholars from the United States and Taiwan collaborate on research and exchange best practices on a range of topics including environmental protection, government accountability, and preventing trafficking in persons. Furthermore, some of the prominent alumni from these programs have included Taiwan's current and previous presidents.

The United States remains committed to supporting Taiwan's confidence and dignity through increased participation in the international community and enhanced security. We continue to support Taiwan's membership in organizations that do not require statehood and to urge meaningful participation in those that do.

At a time when pressure to squeeze Taiwan out of international organizations is growing, we are finding new ways for Taiwan to earn the dignity and respect that its contributions to global challenges merit. In 2015, as a member of the counter-ISIL coalition, Taiwan worked together with the United States to deliver 350 prefabricated homes for displaced families in northern Iraq.

Last June, the American Institute in Taiwan (AIT) and the Taipei Economic and Cultural Representative Office in the United States (TECRO) signed an MOU creating the Global Cooperation and Training Framework, or GCTF – a vehicle for the United States to help showcase Taiwan's strengths and expertise by addressing global and regional concerns. The idea is simple: the United States and Taiwan conduct training programs for experts from throughout the region to assist them with building their own capacities to tackle issues where Taiwan has proven experience and advantages. These include, but are not limited to, women's rights, democratization, global health, and energy security. At the same time, we remain just as committed to Taiwan's meaningful participation in organizations like Interpol, ICAO, WHO, and UNFCCC. We will match Taiwan's growth and innovation with equally innovative approaches to the relationship that highlight Taiwan's contributions to the global community.

On the security front, the United States makes available to Taiwan defense articles and services necessary to enable Taiwan to maintain a sufficient self-defense, which is consistent with our responsibilities under the Taiwan Relations Act. During the Obama administration, we have notified Congress of over $14 billion in arms sales to Taiwan.

Our efforts at supporting Taiwan's self-defense capabilities extend beyond arms sales. We support Taiwan's capacity-building efforts through visits, maintenance programs, and exchanges. Over the last few years, we have nearly doubled the number of our annual security cooperation events, further enabling Taiwan to strengthen its self-defense capabilities.

Due, in part, to these stepped up contacts and strong U.S. partnership, Taipei has gained more confidence in its engagements with Beijing. In recent years, the two sides have pursued constructive dialogue to reach agreements on economic and people-to-people exchanges that promote peace and stability across the Taiwan Strait. Last November, we welcomed the meeting between leaders on both sides of the Taiwan Strait and the historic improvement in cross-Strait relations that it symbolized. Our long-held belief is that cross-Strait differences can and should be resolved peacefully in a manner, pace, and scope acceptable to people on both sides of the Strait.

The United States remains committed to our one-China policy, based on the Three Joint Communiques and the Taiwan Relations Act, a policy that has remained consistent over several decades and over many administrations. The United States has an abiding interest in cross-Strait peace and stability. We will continue to call on both sides to engage in dialogue on the basis of dignity and respect after Taiwan's new administration takes office in May.

During the current transition period, we remain in close contact with the present administration and the incoming administration to encourage both parties to work constructively to ensure a smooth transition and continue to promote peace and stability in the region. We look forward to working with Taiwan's new president and leaders from all parties to further strengthen the unofficial relationship between the United States and the people on Taiwan.

In conclusion, we have developed a vital partnership with Taiwan that is filled with many opportunities for cooperation in the future. We are committed to ensuring that this relationship, built upon the strong foundation of the Taiwan Relations Act, will continue to thrive as we find new innovative ways to deepen our unofficial ties. Taiwan has earned a great deal of respect in the international community, and we will continue to showcase the strengths and benefits of Taiwan's role and contributions in global efforts. The innovative spirit, democratic dynamism, and courageous vision of the people on Taiwan make us proud to be their friend and partner.

Mr. Chairman and Members of the Subcommittee, I would like to thank you again for inviting me to join you today. I am happy to answer any questions.

Mr. SALMON. Thank you, Ms. Thornton.

Regarding the recent earthquake, what kind of assistance are we planning to offer them as they look to find missing people or rebuild?

Ms. THORNTON. Thank you very much, Mr. Chairman, for that question.

We have already in the process of last weekend's earthquake received a declaration of the disaster from the authorities on Taiwan and have responded to that with a contribution that we are making through the Taiwan Red Cross that will go to help the families of those affected by the earthquake.

We have also had a member of our Office of Foreign Disaster Assistance regional team fly to Tainan to inspect the work that was ongoing and to keep coordination with people in the Taiwan authorities to see if there is any additional assistance that would be needed.

So far, the judgment has been made that the Taiwan rescue authorities are fully capable of conducting the onsite rescue. But we are maintaining close contact with them.

Mr. SALMON. Thank you.

In your opening statement at the close, you were reaffirming our commitment to the one-China policy as spelled out in the three communiques and the Taiwan Relations Act and I really appreciate that. I think that is valuable.

Let me just quote—right after Secretary of State John Kerry had his first meeting with his Chinese counterpart, the Foreign Minister, after the elections he said this to reporters:

"Let me just say with respect to one of the issues that the Foreign Minister raised on Taiwan that since they just had an election and a new party has won, the United States does reaffirm the three communiques, which have been the basis of our policy, we remain committed to a one-China policy but we encourage cross-Strait dialogue for resolution of that issue."

Now, in his comments he didn't mention the Taiwan Relations Act, that our one-China policy is not just based on the three communiques but also the Taiwan Relations Act.

As you aptly pointed out, the Taiwan Relations Act states that it is U.S. policy to consider any effort to determine the future of Taiwan by other than peaceful means a threat to peace and security of the Western Pacific area and a grave concern to the United States.

How significant, if at all, do you consider the omission to have been and what if any are the implications?

Ms. THORNTON. Thank you very much, Mr. Chairman.

I would say that Secretary Kerry, in speaking at the press conference, if he omitted the mention of the Taiwan Relations Act in that construct it was certainly unintentional.

We, as a matter of constant practice when we are describing our one-China policy, always try to pair the adherence to the three joint communiques with our strong commitment to the Taiwan Relations Act as a cornerstone of our policy and as, really, the framework within which we conduct our unofficial relationship with Taiwan.

Of course, it also provides for the establishment of the American Institute in Taiwan, which provides for a cadre of experts both in Taiwan and here in Washington, to pursue this relationship with a laser focus on trying to expand our cooperation.

So I want to assure you that Secretary Kerry's omission, if it happened, was completely inadvertent. We have seen President Obama, standing next to President Xi at least twice since I've been in this job at a press conference, mention the Taiwan Relations Act. So I know that it is firmly, you know, part of our——

Mr. SALMON. And we wanted to give you the opportunity to make sure that that was part of the package, that that is a strong commitment and that is a strong part of our policy.

After President Tsai got elected, she said that maintaining the status quo is her commitment to the people of Taiwan regarding the cross-Strait relations and the international community and there won't be provocation and there won't be surprises.

Meanwhile, directly after the election, China broadcast images of archived live-fired military drills. How confident are you, if at all, that the DPP and the Chinese leadership have workable communication channels that might help them avoid misunderstandings and manage the tensions?

Ms. THORNTON. Thank you very much for that very important question.

As you know, in the lead-up to the elections, the United States hosted both of the major Presidential candidates. And in that respect we were able to have a very good conversation with Dr. Tsai about her plans for her administration, about her positions on things like cross-Strait negotiations. And she reaffirmed for us that she is committed to continuing the status quo, that she understands the obligation to continue to pursue a policy that will enable cross-Strait peace and stability and that she intends to work with the authorities in Beijing to try to continue in the manner under which President Ma Ying-jeou has managed to pursue cross-Strait relations.

We also have been, of course, in touch with Chinese officials. As you noted, Secretary Kerry was there just recently meeting with the Foreign Minister and also with President Xi Jinping.

The week before that Deputy Secretary Tony Blinken was also in China meeting with his counterparts and we had a chance in those discussions also to make our very strong desire to see a continuation of cross-Strait stability but also cross-Strait exchanges continue.

We, in those exchanges, counselled restraint, creativity, flexibility in working with the new administration in Taiwan to come up with a basis upon which to continue those negotiations.

And they indicated that they were looking to see what Dr. Tsai was going to propose in that regard. So I am hopeful that they will be able to come up with such a basis for continuing these exchanges.

I think there is a will on both sides to do so.

Mr. SALMON. Thank you.

Mr. Sherman.

Mr. SHERMAN. With the notable exception of our own State Department, every foreign ministry I have talked to—almost everyone—has said that their number-one goal is trade and exports.

And we have a persistent double digit in billions trade deficit with Taiwan. What has the State Department done? What have you personally done to create a circumstance where we are running a trade surplus with Taiwan, at least one that will—a surplus for enough years to the—so that our trade relationship this century will be at a balance?

Ms. THORNTON. Thank you very much, Mr. Congressman, for that question.

And I hope that the State Department has not left you with the misimpression that we are not serious about promoting trade.

Mr. SHERMAN. I will relate to you something that happened in this subcommittee.

The person who—I now mention his name to you privately—probably is the most respected Assistant Ambassador we have had in Asia sat there and said that when he was the Ambassador to South Korea he helped America by putting out on the lawn, and he listed a number of cars that he thought were made in America, and one of the cars he was promoting was 99 percent made in Germany. It had an American nameplate on it.

So and this was someone who hadn't made a stupid mistake in 20 years. Anybody who actually cared about promoting our exports would know whether the car they were trying to get South Koreans to buy was built in America or just labelled in America.

But when you don't care, you know, things fall through the cracks. So yes, indeed, I have a belief that the State—So what have you done, when are we going to get a trade surplus with Taiwan?

Ms. THORNTON. Thank you. Having many years ago worked on auto negotiations with the South Koreans I can well appreciate where you are coming from. But turning to Taiwan, one of the—I mean, I talked a bit in my opening statement about our focus with Taiwan on expanding our economic ties. We work with Taiwan——

Mr. SHERMAN. Yes. We will point out almost always when I talk about the State Department of economic ties, they are more—they are as interested in creating more imports as more exports and I have had State Department officials testify that the trade deficit isn't a problem for American families and that in fact expanding imports is just as wonderful as expanding exports. So please don't talk about trade ties. Talk about exports.

Ms. THORNTON. Okay. I mean, the other thing that the Taiwans have been doing in recent years that we have seen is significant inbound-to-the-United-States investment, creating a lot of U.S. jobs here by building manufacturing plants, by creating ties with technology companies in California, et cetera.

But we work on expanding access—market access for U.S. exports to Taiwan through our Trade and Investment Framework Agreement with Taiwan. This is ongoing intensive dialogue that we have to try to——

Mr. SHERMAN. So we have this intensive dialogue but we're failing every year. Every year we run a trade deficit. Do you know why we are failing? Do you think of it as failure? Or is it success to run a trade deficit?

Ms. THORNTON. No. I mean, this is a constant ongoing problem that we're working on. We are working every year to try to break down additional barriers.

We are working on—for example, this last round in October that Deputy USTR Holleyman led in Taiwan we made some progress on IPR issues that had been posing market barriers to some U.S. exports. We made some progress on pharmaceutical market access on financial services access, so——

Mr. SHERMAN. I am going to reclaim my time. I mean, we are working hard. We are making progress. We are failing every year and we do not have a target date that you can reveal as to when we will reach a trade balance. We will continue to work hard. We will continue to fail.

What additional weapons assistance has Taiwan requested an opportunity to buy in the United States? This is both in the interest of preserving the rights of the Taiwanese people.

I know it is juxtaposed with my question about a trade deficit. Doesn't hurt there either. What have they asked for that we have not green lighted yet?

Ms. THORNTON. Yes, thank you very much for that question.

Mr. SHERMAN. Including what they have asked for informally and you have told them not to ask for formally.

Ms. THORNTON. As I mentioned in my statement, we have sold over $14 billion worth of arms to Taiwan in this administration to date.

We are, of course, making available to Taiwan those articles that are necessary for its self-defense. So we do that in closed consultation with the Taiwanese themselves. And try to base proposals for sales and requests on things——

Mr. SHERMAN. I know all that. Can you answer the question? What are they asking for formally or informally?

Ms. THORNTON. Well, we don't comment actually—yeah, I mean, I can't really comment on ongoing——

Mr. SHERMAN. Will the classified briefing tell me this or will the process of not letting me know be consistent both for——

Ms. THORNTON. I would be happy try to address in more detail in the classified meeting but we don't generally talk about things that are under——

Mr. SHERMAN. Okay. But how are we doing on the F–16s, the mine sweepers? I believe my time has expired. But those are the— I got an answer from my staff. I hope to get an answer from you. Thank you.

Mr. SALMON. Mr. Royce—Chairman Royce.

Mr. ROYCE. Thank you, Mr. Chairman.

You know, one of the issues that I have become concerned about over time is this issue of the lack of regularity or consistency in the discussions between U.S. and Taiwan on the Taiwan Relations Act requirements to provide for the articles for Taiwan's defense needs. I head the legislation to reaffirm the act that passed the House and transferred the four guided missile frigates to Taiwan and I have been down on some of those frigates, one of them, to see it outfitted and so we are moving forward. But there isn't any consistency to

18

this dialogue, and under the act I would interpret it as sort of re-
quiring that. So I would urge the administration to look at that.
But there are a couple aspects of this. When you look at cyber attacks, no country is more targeted than Taiwan and so there is an
area also where the United States, I think, has a certain responsi-
bility to assist in helping Taiwan deter these cyber attacks.

I just give you an opportunity to comment on that, if you want.
And then I know on the discussion to support Taiwan's indigenous
submarine program with the Navy, is there a plan to allow the
U.S. Navy and defense industries here to support Taiwan's indigenous program there?

Ms. THORNTON. Thank you, Mr. Chairman.

I guess what I would mention with regard to the ongoing conversations in the defense area, I mean, we have more than doubled
the number of sort of working level contacts that we have with Taiwan in this space.

We also have, under the Obama administration and, you know,
which is coincident, of course, with the administration of Ma Ying-
jeou in Taiwan we have also increased markedly the number of
high-level exchanges that we've had back and forth. And on the defense sector in particular, I think I would prefer to respond to your
questions in detail in the closed session.

But let me assure you that we are working with Taiwan very
closely on all of the issues that you raise.

Mr. ROYCE. And the F–16 issue that Mr. Sherman also raised,
I think, is also of concern.

One of the objectives that I think we have all had who have
looked at Taiwan's economic strength is that its inclusion in TPP
would allow Taiwan greater diversification in terms of its exports
of Kaohsiung and Tainan. You know, you see what they produce
and also would allow for greater imports around the Pacific Rim
and also, obviously, if Taiwan gets a seat at the table for the second round you could also help Taiwan protect its long-term interests should we do a trans-Atlantic agreement with Europe because
then it could be folded in eventually, if it's folded into the Pacific
Rim.

I assume the long-term goal here, as I understand it, is an agreement with very high standards and a high standard agreement
serves the interest of the United States. There are really two different competing theories on liberalized trade.

One theory—for those who believe in trade—one theory is that
you will try to drive policies of free trade and no standards. The
United States doesn't benefit under that.

We benefit under the rule of law, the establishment of the rule
of law. And in Taipei also, Taiwan is advantaged by high standard
agreement.

Increasingly, as we travel—and I think we've had four trips of
our delegation to Asia in the last 3 years—we hear this feedback
across southeast Asia and east Asia that, you know, somebody
needs to be pushing this concept to very high standards on intellectual property protections and all the indigenous innovation, all
these issues that we're mutually concerned about and that the Eu-
ropeans are also concerned about.

And if we get a major trans-Atlantic and Pacific Rim agreement we will have the ability to enforce that.

But if Taiwan doesn't have that seat at the table and doesn't get to diversify its imports and exports, then I think this would be problematic. That is why I keep encouraging our administration and the government to move forward on getting the base bilateral investment agreement done.

How do things look on that front?

Ms. THORNTON. Well, thank you very much, Mr. Chairman.

We do know, of course, that Taiwan has expressed interest in joining high standards trade agreements, regional agreements in part because it is so good at enforcing and holds itself up to a high rule of law standards, also because of the concern that they have about diversification of their economy, wanting to ensure that they are integrated into the region and also that they expand their network of trading partners so they don't become overdependent on one particular trading partner, and we certainly support that objective, generally, that strategic objective that they have.

As far as sort of our working with them, what we have said is that we want to work with them to get them ready to exceed to a high standard trade and investment agreement in the future and that is what we have been doing for the Trade and Investment Framework Agreement is they have already recognized that they have certain structural changes that they need to make in order to move in that direction. And we have told them that we will be happy to help them with that first by working on some of the structural and market access barriers that they already have that are going to be an impediment to them joining these high standards trade agreements, and then further down the road helping them to prepare for that.

Mr. ROYCE. Thank you, Ms. Thornton.

Thank you, Mr. Chairman.

Mr. SALMON. Thank you.

Mr. Connolly.

Mr. CONNOLLY. Thank you, Mr. Chairman.

And let me begin by besides welcoming you, Ms. Thornton, agreeing with Chairman Royce. We need a high standard liberalized trade regime and I would add, and I know the chairman would agree, three more words—enforceable and enforced—because only then is free trade credible here at home and abroad.

But in my view, there is no question that our helping to set those high standards is far preferable to the alternative in the Trans-Pacific Region and I certainly look forward to supporting the agreement.

Taiwan, Ms. Thornton, should it be—if it asks should it be incarnated into the TPP? What is the U.S. position? Could you speak into the mic a little?

Ms. THORNTON. Yes. So, I mean, our position has been to welcome Taiwan's interest in the TPP and, as I mentioned in response to the chairman's question, to let them know that they have a number of things that they need to do to prepare and get ready to accede to a high standards trade agreement and that we are willing to work with them on sort of moving ahead on reforms that they need to make in order to be ready and make themselves an attractive partner for other members in those high standards——

Mr. CONNOLLY. But what I hear you saying is, given its status, the U.S. position is not to exclude its potential membership in the TPP.

Ms. THORNTON. That is not our position, correct.

Mr. CONNOLLY. Okay. You would agree that the Taiwan Relations Act of 1979 codifies the relationship with Taiwan post recognition of China and included in that codification is a defensive military support framework, correct?

U.S. is committed to providing defensive military support, correct?

Ms. THORNTON. Well, there is——I mean, it is very clear in the TRA but yes, we are committed to providing defensive articles to maintain Taiwan's self defense.

Mr. CONNOLLY. Now, Taiwan has requested, among other items, mine sweeping capability, F–16 combat aircraft, diesel submarines and frigates, which we are providing.

How long ago did Taiwan make those defensive military requests to the United States Government?

Ms. THORNTON. I am going to have to defer, I think, this to the closed session. I am sorry.

Mr. CONNOLLY. No, it is a matter of public record, Ms. Thornton. It is not a matter of closed anything.

When, for the record, did Taiwan ask for those——that equipment? There's nothing classified about it. Been in the newspapers. And by the way, that hearing has been cancelled so you can't——I'm not going to let you do that. I mean, I wouldn't ask you a classified question. It's not classified. Matter of public record.

Ms. THORNTON. There are stories in the media about things that Taiwan desires to procure from the United States but as far as——

Mr. CONNOLLY. The question was when did they first request these equipment——this equipment.

Ms. THORNTON. To my knowledge, some of these things have not been requested formally.

Mr. CONNOLLY. Evasive, Ms. Thornton. Did Taiwan——let's pick one. How long ago did Taiwan——because we do know this one——ask for diesel submarines?

Could the clock——Mr. Chairman, could I just ask the indulgence of the chair while apparently the witnesses have to consult?

Ms. THORNTON. So yes, my assist from the rear says that we announced in April 2001 that we were going to cooperate with Taiwan on developing a plan for diesel submarines.

Mr. CONNOLLY. Thank you. Okay. Fifteen years ago. Why has it taken 15 years to adjudicate that request, one way or the other? Kind of a long time, wouldn't you think?

Ms. THORNTON. It is a long time and we've been working on it for 15 years and we're continuing to work on it today.

Mr. CONNOLLY. Oh, well. We're all reassured, Ms. Thornton.

Well, let me just say for Members of Congress I think on both sides of the aisle it does raise questions about who's making U.S. policy and who's writing the answers to legitimate defensive military requests from the Government of Taiwan pursuant to a statute that you yourself just acknowledged does indeed undergird the relationship.

And included in that statute is a codification of our support for defensive military equipment to ensure that whatever the ultimate resolution is in the Taiwan Strait is a peaceful one and I think you—would you not agree that a 15-year wait for any answer on any item on that list seems to be an awfully long time?

Ms. THORNTON. I certainly agree that it's a long time but I'll just say that it is complicated and that I could go into more detail in the closed session if we ever have that opportunity.

Mr. CONNOLLY. I appreciate that. But we do understand this complication but, you know, the king of Siam used to say it's a puzzlement. But 15 years—my goodness.

Okay. Final question, if I may, Mr. Chairman. What is the U.S. position with respect to Taiwan joining, being accepted into international organizations? Do we support that bid?

Ms. THORNTON. Yes. We support Taiwan's membership in international organizations where statehood is not a requirement for membership and we support their active participation in organizations where they do require statehood for membership.

Mr. CONNOLLY. Do we support Taiwan's bid to be a member of Interpol?

Ms. THORNTON. We support Taiwan's active participation in Interpol and we have been working on that.

Mr. CONNOLLY. Status to be determined?

Ms. THORNTON. Yeah. I mean—yeah.

Mr. CONNOLLY. Okay. Got it. Because obviously that's one that's very practical irrespective of status and we want more cooperation.

Thank you very much. Mr. Chairman, thank you for the time.

Mr. SALMON. Mr. Chabot.

Mr. CHABOT. Thank you, Mr. Chairman.

Ms. Thornton, let me follow up on my colleague from the Commonwealth of Virginia, Mr. Connolly, on the submarine and defense issues in general.

As a former chairman of this committee and as one of the cofounders of congressional Taiwan caucus and a long time friend of Taiwan, my recollection is with respect to the submarines in particular.

One of the problems is nobody makes diesel submarines any more, that we know. I think there was some talk about maybe the French could still do it but that was one of the problems, you know, with nuclear submarines.

But in order—because of the expense, the fact that you don't necessarily need nuclear submarines in that part of the world, et cetera, that diesel—in fact, I saw the—I guess they have a World War II era submarine out there.

I think it was down at the naval base in Kaohsiung, I believe is where I saw that—I've seen a few nodding of heads in the audience with folks who know a lot more out this than I do.

But in any event, I know that was one of the problems. But here is my question to you about this whole thing. You know, the planes and the anti-missile system and the submarines, improving the defensive abilities of Taiwan in case the PRC did decide to get even more belligerent and hostile than they have been over the last couple of decades, it's critical that Taiwan does strengthen their military and their defenses.

But one of the problems—you know, we had a hard time getting this stuff through here but when we finally did we ran into a roadblock with Taiwan because even though you had a DPP President, President Chen Shui-bian, who wanted to move ahead with this, you've had KMT who has controlled the legislature, you know, since martial law, I believe.

Is that correct? And Speaker Wong, I think, would try to get it through the legislature and just couldn't get it. When we weren't willing to act, you know, they wanted it and when we finally got around to doing it then they couldn't get it through there, and I'm seeing some nods from some of your assistant folks here too.

So is that one of the issues that we face? And then I guess the real question is this. We just had a pretty important election in Taiwan recently and the DPP now is not only going to have the presidency but they're also going to control the Legislative Yuan for the first time ever.

So is there maybe some light at the end of the tunnel in actually getting this defense that Taiwan so desperately needs and actually make it happen? Do you want to comment on it?

Ms. THORNTON. Thank you. Yeah, no, no. That's an excellent comment and thank you for the question.

You know, we certainly work very closely with the Taiwan side to make sure that the capabilities that we're providing are augmenting its asymmetric and innovative security approach.

And so within that we have to look at different systems and see which things are going to make the most sense for what Taiwan needs.

It is true that the expenditures that they have to dedicate to these capabilities do, you know, have to be factored in on the Taiwan side and I'll just note that, you know, $14 billion in arms sales over the last several years is a considerable amount to absorb and to, you know, to fund through their defense budget.

Of course, Taiwan has also recently gone to an all-volunteer force, which has also expanded its personnel costs and caused it to need to do some restructuring of its budget so——

Mr. CHABOT. If I could cut you off there for just a minute. I have only got 1 minute left. I had two more things I wanted to ask you real quickly. If I could get a quick response.

Can you think of any other countries that we deal with that we bar their top four leaders from coming to our capital, Washington, DC?

Ms. THORNTON. I am not sure. But I just want to point out on that note that we have actually—you know, we have Presidential transits for the safety, dignity, comfort and security of the traveler. We had the Vice——

Mr. CHABOT. Right. They can go to—they can go to San Francisco, they can go to New York.

Ms. THORNTON [continuing]. Vice Premier in California earlier this year.

Mr. CHABOT. President Tsai isn't going to be able to come here to Washington, DC, unless we change our policy. Is that correct?

Ms. THORNTON. That has been the policy.

Mr. CHABOT. We ought to change our policy.

And then finally, I got 10 seconds left. President Chen Shui-bian was finally released about a year ago on medical parole. How is he doing?

Ms. THORNTON. As far as I understand, he's doing well and he's still on medical parole as far as I know.

Mr. CHABOT. Thank you very much. I yield back my time.

Ms. MENG. Ms. Thornton, there is a sense that part of the momentum toward President-elect Tsai's election was a response to a slowing of Taiwan's economy, particularly with exports and imports.

President-elect Tsai has specifically mentioned plans to have a closer economic relationship with the United States.

However, U.S. businesses in Taiwan report facing inadequate or outdated laws, government bureaucracy, inconsistent regulatory interpretations and a lack of regulatory transparency, et cetera, as barriers to further economic development.

What is your sense of the political will of President-elect Tsai and the newly-elected DPP majority in the Legislative Yuan to address these issues directly?

Ms. THORNTON. Thank you very much for that question.

In our conversations with Dr. Tsai and with her team, it is my sense that this is an area that she is very well aware of that is inhibiting Taiwan's economic potential and that she is looking to move as a priority once she takes office to try to address.

And we have been very keen to work with her under—in the new administration, again, through our Trade and Investment Framework Agreement process which her team is well aware of and has been briefed on to try to move forward on some of the intractable market access barriers that we've seen in Taiwan and also some of these regulatory problems that do create a lot of constraints for our businesses and our potential investors.

Ms. MENG. And my second question on a different topic, our relation to the South China Sea. How do recent reports of possible joint naval patrols by the U.S. and India in the South China Sea work into the U.S.'s priority to de-escalate tensions there?

Ms. THORNTON. Yes. I can't really comment on the story about the joint patrols between the U.S. and India. As far as I am aware, there is no concrete plan in that regard.

But certainly the U.S. policy for the South China Sea is to call on all of the claimants and regional players to try to reduce tensions, to preserve freedom of navigation and overflight and to try to resolve disputes peacefully and conduct themselves in accordance with the rule of law.

And I don't—so I don't think that there's a—I mean, our presence in that part of the world has been longstanding. It's a part of our security presence in that region, which has helped maintain peace and stability in Asia for—ever since the second—end of the second World War and I think we don't see any problem with patrols or other things that are in keeping with freedom of flight and freedom of navigation.

Ms. MENG. Thank you. I yield back.

Mr. SALMON. Thank you, Ms. Meng.

That will conclude the first panel.

We will have the second panel be seated. I just also wanted to say that we are trying to reschedule the classified briefing because we are going to have votes called in about 15 minutes.

We might just get through the testimony of the second panel when we get called for votes. But thank you so much, Ms. Thornton, for coming and thank you for all your attention. So we'll seat the next panel now.

I think we'll go ahead and move on with introductions. I know we're kind of clearing the room out but we want to make sure we get your testimony before we have to go vote.

We are really pleased to be joined today by three excellent panelists. First, Mr. Randall Schriver, president and CEO of the Project 2049 Institute; Ms. Bonnie Glaser, good to see you again, senior advisor for Asia and director of the China Power Project and Center for Strategic and International Studies; and Dr. Shelley Rigger, Davidson University's political science department.

We are really grateful for these witnesses joining us today to lend their expertise and we'll start with you, Mr. Schriver.

STATEMENT OF MR. RANDALL SCHRIVER, PRESIDENT AND CHIEF EXECUTIVE OFFICER, PROJECT 2049 INSTITUTE

Mr. SCHRIVER. Thank you, Mr. Chairman, very much appreciate the invitation and I appreciate being seated alongside Dr. Rigger and Ms. Glaser, who I have enormous respect for as well.

I want to join others who express condolences and thoughts and prayers. Certainly, it's a difficult time and we wish them well in the recovery efforts.

It's a very timely hearing, as has been noted, due to the recent election and I think it's appropriate that we acknowledge the significance of this event.

It's a young democracy. They are under tremendous pressure. So just carrying out a free and fair election is something worthy of our praise.

In your instructions you asked me to speak specifically about economic and trade issues, which I will do. Before doing that I think it's also appropriate to note President Ma and the fact that he's coming to the end of his tenure.

He's been a great friend of the United States, has done a terrific job promoting peace and stability in the region, I think often not given credit for his South China Sea peace initiative—the East China Sea peace initiative.

So as we move into a new administration we should reflect on his accomplishments. Dr. Tsai is somebody who's very experienced on trade matters. She herself has been a trade negotiator and I think she campaigned on economic reform and promoting trade. I think that gives us opportunities that we would be very smart to seize upon.

As mentioned by others, she has a keen interest in joining TPP. I'm of the view that we should not only welcome that interest but be very clear that we want Taiwan in a second round, should there be one, and I hope there is, and that we will work with them to identify a clear pathway to entry.

I listened carefully to the administration statement. We welcome their interest. I believe we should welcome more than their interest. I think we should work with them to have a concrete path to inclusion in TPP.

I agree with previous comments made about the investment environment and the need for a bilateral investment agreement. Taiwan is a significant investor in the United States and, of course, vice versa.

That can be strengthened. There are too many barriers still in place so we should keep these delegations going but more to the point work through the various fora to try to create a better environment for mutual investment.

I think there are other areas of our economic relationship that could also be strengthened. I think defense industrial cooperation is something we should consider.

There were, I think, some very good questions about the submarine program—why 15 years. Certainly, if Taiwan does determine to go the path of an indigenous diesel electric submarine, there are opportunities for our industry to get involved in that and I think the administration could send clear signals that we welcome that kind of defense industrial cooperation and it could really give a boost to this program and maybe it won't be another 15 years until we see a submarine there in Taiwan.

I think in the S & T area as well this has been one of the past areas of success. Taiwan is a very innovative country. They are a global leader in patents and, to use an overused phrase, there are a lot of win-win opportunities, I think, if we really strengthen our S & T cooperation not only in defense but beyond that and into that high-tech sector.

This is all going to unfold under an environment where I expect there to be increasing pressure, not only military pressure in the missiles that we're all aware of but there are rumors that China is preparing for a more coercive path, cutting back tours, cutting back flights, et cetera.

We can do these things irrespective of the positions China takes but, of course, it becomes more challenging, at least politically and diplomatically, to do that in face of more pressure.

But I think we have to remember to keep the onus on Beijing. They are the ones who have a policy that's failing. They're the ones that have the military posture opposite Taiwan, threatening them and intimating the people there and they are the ones that also need to show some flexibility

So people regard this election as a potential inflection point but we need to remember that the real core of the problem is Beijing's intransigence and the positions that they're taking.

So just to conclude very briefly, I think there are five things. I think TPP in a very clear path is important. I think more on bilateral investment to include not only the bilateral agreement but the promotion of these delegations. I think on the defense side, there is much more that can be done and I think several of the systems were mentioned—F–16s, mine sweepers. But I have a particular interest in the submarine program because I think there's an opportunity for defense industrial cooperation. The S & T area is a fourth area I think is very promising and then finally in our diplomacy keep some balance. This election is one of the reasons we're here talking. But if you pull that thread too far some people might be oriented toward blaming democracy or blaming Taiwan for the instability.

The problem is in Beijing and we need to keep that in mind as we go forward and continue to put our emphasis on their need to de-escalate, to demilitarize and to have some flexibility.

Thank you, Mr. Chairman.

[The prepared statement of Mr. Schriver follows:]

Testimony of Randall G. Schriver

Founding Partner, Armitage International
President & CEO, The Project 2049 Institute

February 11, 2015
House Committee on Foreign Affairs

Mr. Chairman and esteemed committee members, I would like to express my appreciation for the opportunity to appear before your committee to discussfutureprospects for U.S.-Taiwan relations, an issue vital to U.S. interests and peace and stability in the Asia-Pacific region.

Given recent events in Taiwan, I would be remiss not to take a moment to acknowledge the victims of last week's earthquake. We in the U.S. should keep Taiwan in our thoughts and prayers as rescue and recovery continuein the coming weeks.

Taiwan's successful election this year was a significant milestonein deepening Taiwan's democracy, and Taiwan deserves our recognition and praise for continuing to be an example of a thriving democracy in Asia. As a still "young" democracy, and as a country that faces coercion and pressure from the People's Republic of China, these events should not be taken for granted.

It is also appropriate as President Ma's term of service approaches an end that we reflect on his significant accomplishments. Too often overlooked in the United States,we should note his efforts at peacemaking and diplomacy in the East China Sea and South China Sea, reaching agreements to end maritime disputes with Japan and the Philippines, and furthering peace and stability in the cross-Strait relationship.

Per your guidance, my testimony today will focus on trade and economic issues in the U.S.-Taiwan relationship, and prospects for strengthening the relationship post-election. U.S. support for Taiwan has served as a symbol of U.S. commitment to peace and security in the Asia-Pacific region, and Taiwan is an important strategic and economic partner that can help advance U.S. interests in the region. The U.S. has an important strategic interest in the health of Taiwan's economy as we seek a region that promotes a liberal political order and free trade. Strengthening trade and economic cooperation between the U.S. and Taiwan is therefore a critical aspect of continuing to develop this important relationship.

U.S.-Taiwan Trade and Economic Relationship:

Though the U.S. and Taiwan have enjoyed successful cooperation over a wide range of economic, security, and diplomatic issues, the strong trade relationship alone demonstrates the importance of Taiwan for U.S. interests. Despite its relatively small population of 23 million, Taiwan is the United States' 10th largest trading partner, 14th largest export market for U.S. goods, and 12th largest source of imports. U.S. companies, Taiwan's largest source of foreign investment, areheavily invested in the manufacturing, finance and insurance, and wholesale trade sectors. Taiwanese companies are also heavily invested in the United States, as cumulative investment reached $13.93 billion in 2015.

President-elect Tsai Ing-wen and the DPP campaign prioritized economic reform in response to growing Taiwanese frustration with a stagnating economy and a relatively high unemployment rate. Particularly, Tsai promised to seek greater diversification among trading partners as the Taiwanese public has grown more and more concerned about Taiwan's growing economic dependence on China. Dr. Tsai plans on reinvigorating the economy by strengthening local industries, reducing Taiwan's dependence on China, and expanding global trade.

The United States should seize this opportunity to expand its trade relationship with Taiwan and promote Taiwan's further integration into the global economy. Tsai Ing-wen has expressed keen interest in joining the TPP, making it a cornerstone of her campaign. As the 26th largest economy in the world, inclusion of Taiwan would significantly enhance the trade pact. A recent study estimates that Taiwan's accession to the TPP will generate over $20 billion of welfare gains for the twelve parties. As the TPP is a fundamental component of a successful rebalance strategy, the U.S. must ensure that Taiwan is included. It is my hope that the United States and its partners in the TPP will conclude the current round with full ratification of the agreement, and then move quickly to launch a second round of negotiations with an eye toward expansion. Taiwan should be a part of the second-round talks, along with South Korea and perhaps other interested nations.

In the event that there is not timely movement on TPP, the U.S. should consider a bilateral free trade agreement with Taiwan. Our Trade and Investment Framework Agreement (TIFA) should be leveraged further to pursue robust bilateral trade liberalization. In fact, these efforts can be made in parallel with ongoing discussions on TPP. Genuine efforts toward a bilateral FTA will ultimately assist all parties in pursuing multilateral trade liberalization in the future.

US-Taiwan Defense Industrial Cooperation:

Another emerging area of economic cooperation is in the area of defense industrial cooperation. Such cooperation not only supports the broader U.S. goals surrounding our interest in strengthening Taiwan's defense, but it also makes economic sense for both countries. While some critics point to the need for Taiwan to raise its defense budget, many of those same analysts ignore one of the most promising avenues for enhancing Taiwan's defense capabilities – defense industrial cooperation associated with direct commercial sales of military equipment and services. Trade-offs between expenditures on national defense, economic growth, and social welfare are often contested, not only in Taiwan but in other societies as well. Defense spending, given the proper set of circumstances, can contribute to economic growth and development. The creation of jobs and income at the local level in Taiwan, along with technology spin-offs, could increase support for greater defense spending. As long as Taiwan's defense industry remains weak, public support for a larger defense budget is likely to be inadequate. This is especially true when faced with what is known as a "crowding out" effect. With legal caps on deficit spending, an increase in defense expenditure incurs opportunity costs, displacing spending in other sectors, such as education, social welfare, S&T, and investment into economic infrastructure. Along these lines, a consensus exists in favor of major indigenous programs, such as diesel electric submarines. Fair consideration of export licenses and other forms of technical assistance in support of Taiwan's indigenous submarine program is warranted.

U.S.-Taiwan Science & Technology (S&T) Cooperation:

Beyond trade, Tsai Ing-wen's election will also present other opportunities to partner with Taiwan. The Taiwanese economy has long relied upon maintaining a technological comparative advantage, and sustaining this advantage is an important driving force shaping the future of the region. The U.S. and Taiwan share a long history of S&T cooperation since a 1967 agreement between ROC Vice President Yen Chia-Kan and President Lyndon Johnson to make S&T cooperation a priority in the relationship. Recent cooperation has involved technical information exchanges, atmospheric research, water resources development, meteorology and forecast systems development, and other areas. Researchers from Taiwan and the U.S. have also partnered on environmental and natural disaster research, such as the ongoing space collaboration on the COSMIC-2/FORMOSAT-7 program, which works to improve weather forecasting abilities. The Taiwanese Environmental Protection Agency has worked with the U.S. EPA for over 20 years to collaborate on environmental protection issues important to both sides. Taiwan is included in the United States' International Environmental Partnership Program (IEP), which shares best practices on environmental issues with countries around the world. The U.S. and Taiwan could deepen and broaden their economic relationship by expanding S&T cooperation.Additionally, S&T cooperation could help Taiwan maintain its technological advantage and produce mutually beneficial innovations.

Cross-Strait Relations:

Much (if not all) of what is described above can be pursued irrespective of China's views. However, we'd be wise to prepare for an environment in which Beijing puts increasing pressure on Taipei and Washington to curb bilateral cooperation. Since 2008, Taiwan and China have established direct commercial flights, promoted bilateral tourism and signed an Economic Cooperative Framework Agreement (ECFA). Notably, in November 2015 Ma Ying-jeou met with Xi Jinping in Singapore, the first meeting of leaders from both sides of the Strait since 1949.

However, even as Taiwan and China develop their political and economic relationship, China still poses an enormous security challenge to Taiwan. Beijing refuses to renounce the use of force against Taiwan, and maintains a threatening posture against the people on Taiwan. China's military modernization has significantly improved its power and advantages over Taiwan. According to U.S. and Taiwanese analysts, China has more than 1,500 missiles targeting Taiwan. The PLA has developed other military capabilities in the areas of electronic warfare, counter-space, and undersea warfare. Ultimately, Chinese military leaders seek capabilities that could support an attempt to invade and physically occupy Taipei.

Security ties between the U.S. and Taiwan continue to be a fundamental component of the relationship as well. Guided by the Taiwan Relations Act (TRA), the U.S. is committed to providing Taiwan with arms according to its defensive needs. This commitment should be the hallmark of our defense relationship with Taiwan, but in recent years the United States has neglected its obligations. As the PRC continues its military buildup intended to intimidate Taiwan, the United States should avoid allowing pressure from China to keep it from fulfilling this commitment. After a four year absence of arms sales notifications to Taiwan, the December 2015 sale was a positive, albeit modest step. The Obama Administration and the succeeding administration need to take bolder steps to demonstrate their strong support for Taiwan. Taiwan is too often approached as an "issue to manage" within the context of U.S.-China relations, rather than as a valuable economic and strategic partner. Resuming regular arms sales and increasing our support for Taiwan's defense is the best way to demonstrate our commitment to this relationship.

In addition to military pressure, China is also increasing its efforts to employ economic and diplomatic coercion. Beijing's strategy is to isolate Taiwan from the rest of the world. The United States should closely monitor China's reaction to the election and power transition. China is likely to step up efforts to impose economic pressure on Taiwan. Supporting trade with Taiwan and expanding its integration into the global economy is not simply an economic tool; it is a strategic tool. Through trade with Taiwan, the U.S. can ensure the survival of Taiwan's democracy, free market economy, and continued existence as a responsible regional and global actor.

China has already taken some steps to put more pressure on Taiwan. In December 2015, it was announced that China's Tsinghua Unigroup would buy significant shares of two Taiwanese semiconductor and testing and packaging companies, a sign of China's ambition to compete with Taiwan in the chip industry. Since the election, there has been speculation that China will reduce the number of tourists allowed to visit Taiwan as well as the number of flights from the mainland to Taiwan.There is also speculation that Beijing will end the so-called "diplomatic truce" and will attempt to bribe Taiwan's diplomatic partners to switch diplomatic recognition to the People's Republic of China. And it is widely believed Beijing will seek to rollback the few gains Taiwan has made in the area of international space. It is in our interest to help Taiwan in its efforts to resist this type of marginalization and quarantine.

Policy Recommendations

There are several ways the U.S. can strengthenour relationship with Taiwan.

First, the U.S. should champion Taiwan's candidacy for TPP and work to identify a concrete, early path to TPP for Taiwan.

Second, the U.S. should continue to support reciprocal delegations for investment promotion. In the past, Taiwan has sent delegations of investors and business leaders to the United States to demonstrate its commitment to trade and investment with the United States. The U.S. could sponsor a similar delegation to Taiwan to explore investment and business opportunities between the two sides.

Third, the U.S. should address Taiwan's security gaps. The Obama Administration has an opportunity to announce another major arms package before they leave office. Failing this, I'd urge a new U.S. Administration to approve an early arms package to include modern fighter aircraft and concrete support for diesel electric submarines.

Fourth, the U.S. should become more creative in promoting our economic ties with Taiwan by reinvigorating S&T cooperation, and by endorsing and supporting robust defense industrial cooperation.

And fifth, the U.S. should keep the onus on Beijing for maintaining peace and stability in the Taiwan Strait, and for improving cross-Strait ties. Our diplomacy must strenuously reject Chinese attempts to intimate, coerce and isolate the people of Taiwan. In particular, early efforts should be made to continue assisting Taiwan in its legitimate quest for greater international space. We all benefit from Taiwan's continued participation in the World Health Assembly, and we'd all better off with Taiwan as a full an active member of the International Civil Aviation Organization.

Taiwan's recent elections and upcoming leadership transition present an excellent opportunity to improve our trade and economic relationship with Taiwan, just one way the U.S. can demonstrate its commitment to Taiwan's success as a democracy and free market economy. As a flourishing democracy, thriving economy, and a long-standing security partner in East Asia, Taiwan possesses intrinsic value for the United States, and should be viewed as an important partner in a successful U.S. rebalance to the Asia-Pacific.

I hope the Obama Administration and friends in Congress will share this outlook. Thank you again Mr. Chairman for the opportunity to participate in your hearing today, and to offer these thoughts.

Mr. SALMON. Thank you.

Ms. Glaser.

STATEMENT OF MS. BONNIE GLASER, SENIOR ADVISER FOR ASIA, DIRECTOR OF CHINA POWER PROJECT, CENTER FOR STRATEGIC AND INTERNATIONAL STUDIES

Ms. GLASER. Thank you, Chairman Salmon, Ranking Member Sherman and distinguished members of the committee. I too would like to offer my thoughts and prayers to the people of Taiwan as they recover from this earthquake.

The United States has a deep and abiding interest in the preservation of Taiwan's security and democracy. The Taiwan Relations Act remains an important touchstone for Congress, for policy makers and the executive branch and to ensure Taiwan's security the U.S. Government must actively seek to use all the tools of U.S. policy and implement not only the letter but also the spirit and the intentions behind the TRA.

I have been asked to address my remarks to Taiwan's security and the threats to Taiwan's security are numerous and they are growing.

Efforts to sustain the island's economic prosperity which is a critically important component of national security are facing challenges.

Taiwan is largely excluded from the Asia Pacific regional economic integration process. The U.S. can and should do more to advocate for Taiwan's increased participation in international organizations and especially those that would enhance the safety and welfare of Taiwan's citizens and I commend Chairman Salmon for introducing the legislation that urges the Obama administration to support Taiwan's efforts to obtain observer status in Interpol from which it was expelled in 1984.

Without question the greatest and most direct threat to Taiwan's security is, of course, posed by the Chinese military. U.S. security assistance including but not limited to arms sales to Taiwan is vital to deter China from coercing or attacking Taiwan and to enable Taiwan's armed forces to fight effectively in all possible contingencies.

Cooperation with China reviewing presents important opportunities for the United States, for example, to reverse global warming and prevent nuclear proliferation, and the U.S., of course, should seek to work with Beijing to address regional and global challenges where possible.

However, it is harmful to American interests to be so eager for Chinese cooperation that it appears willing to sacrifice Taiwan for better U.S.-China ties. Such an approach sends the wrong signal to Beijing.

It creates anxiety in Taiwan and it fosters doubt throughout the region about America's willingness to withstand Chinese pressure in support of its commitments.

The KMT defeat in the election Tsai Ing-wen created some uncertainty about the future of cross-Strait relations. The mainland insists that Tsai Ing-wen accept its definition of the existing political foundation, which is essentially opposition to Taiwan independence and support of the 1992 consensus.

Tsai Ing-wen has recently defined this existing political foundation differently. For her, it includes a historical fact of the 1992 talks, the prevailing Republic of China constitutional order, the accumulated outcome of more than 20 years of cross-Strait interaction and importantly democratic principles and the will of the Taiwanese people.

The U.S. Government can play a role, I believe, to help narrow the gap between mainland China and Taiwan by encouraging each side to provide assurances to the other to assuage their respective fears.

The U.S. should strongly discourage Beijing from using coercive measures to pressure Tsai and the DPP to concede to its demands.

Punitive actions by China could compel Tsai Ing-wen to respond and perhaps result in a negative spiral that could produce a cross-Strait setback and even a crisis.

Beijing appears to be deliberating how to respond to the DPP's return to power in Taiwan. I think the Xi Jinping has not yet made a decision. But if he adopts the more coercive and even aggressive approach to Taiwan, the U.S. response will be widely viewed as an indicator of the credibility of American commitments.

And not only Japan but also countries in Southeast Asia would be alarmed if Washington fails to provide to Taiwan in the face of Chinese coercion or aggression.

For more than two decades the U.S. has insisted the decisions about Taiwan's future must have the assent of the people of Taiwan in a democratic manner and public opinion polls show that a majority of the people of Taiwan yes, they favor talks with mainland China but dwindling numbers favor reunification. In 2015, a record low of 9.1 percent of respondents in Taiwan favoured unification either now or in the future.

And this polling data, combined with the outcome of the election, suggests that there could be a realignment of political forces and attitudes underway in Taiwan and it is imperative that the U.S. help Taiwan to preserve the autonomy that its people desire and ensure that the differences between Taipei and Beijing be managed peacefully.

Thank you.

[The prepared statement of Ms. Glaser follows:]

Statement before the

House Foreign Affairs Committee

Subcommittee on Asia and the Pacific

"The Future of U.S.-Taiwan Relations"

A Testimony by:

Bonnie S. Glaser

Senior Advisor for Asia and

Director, China Power Project

Center for Strategic and International Studies (CSIS)

February 11, 2016

2200 Rayburn House Office Building

Chairman Salmon, Ranking Member Sherman and Distinguished Members of the Subcommittee:

The US relationship with Taiwan is extremely important to the United States and to the US position in the Asia-Pacific region. The sub-committee on the Asia-Pacific is making an important contribution to American interests by holding these hearings today. Thank you for the opportunity to serve as a witness.

Last month Taiwan held its sixth direct election of the president by the citizens of Taiwan. Tsai Ing-wen of the Democratic Progressive Party (DPP) was elected president with 56% of the vote. For the first time ever, the DPP secured a majority in the legislature, winning 68 of 133 seats. This marks the third peaceful transfer of power through direct elections in Taiwan, and is a further validation of the vitality of Taiwan's democracy. Taiwan is the only ethnic Chinese society in the world that holds a competitive popular election to select its top leader. Taiwan's democracy serves as an example and an inspiration to others, including the People's Republic of China. As President George W. Bush noted in his congratulatory message to Ma Ying-jeou and the people of Taiwan in 2008, "Taiwan is a beacon of democracy to Asia and the world."

Regardless of which political party is in power in Taiwan, the United States has a deep and abiding interest in the preservation of Taiwan's security and democracy. US commitments to Taiwan are laid out the Taiwan Relations Act of 1979, which created the basis for continuing substantive relations with Taiwan in the absence of formal diplomatic ties and set out crucial policy and political commitments. The TRA is an important touchstone for the US Congress and policy makers in the executive branch. To ensure Taiwan's security, the US government must actively seek to use all the tools of US policy to implement not only the letter, but also the spirit and intentions behind the TRA.

Threats to Taiwan's national security are numerous and growing. Efforts to sustain the island's economic prosperity, a critically important component of national security, are facing challenges. Taiwan is largely excluded from the Asia-Pacific regional economic integration process. Marginalization from trade pacts not only puts Taiwan's exports at a disadvantage, it also reduces pressure on Taiwan to undertake needed domestic reforms to increase economic competitiveness Taiwan's security is also threatened by its exclusion from key international organizations. For example, Taiwan is unable to receive timely information on criminals and possible terrorist threats because it has no access to the International Criminal Police Organization's (Interpol) system of alerts and its database on criminals. Although Taiwan's government makes every effort to adhere to international nuclear nonproliferation and safety standards, it is kept out of all international bodies and multilateral meetings that govern nuclear nonproliferation and nuclear security.

The United States can and should do more to advocate for Taiwan's increased participation in international organizations, especially those that would enhance the safety and welfare of Taiwan's citizens as well as regional and global security. I commend Chairman Matt Salmon for introducing legislation that urges the US government to support Taiwan's efforts to obtain observer status in Interpol. In the face of growing threats from epidemics such as Ebola and the Zika virus, further enhancing Taiwan's role in the World Health Organization would avail other countries of Taiwan's world class medical capabilities and ensure Taiwan has timely access to medical information.

Without question, the greatest and most direct threat to Taiwan's security is posed by the Chinese military. China has refused to renounce the use of force against Taiwan. The Anti-Secession Law that was passed by China's National People's Congress in 2005 provides a legal justification, under certain circumstances, for attacking Taiwan. The PLA continues to develop and deploy military capabilities to coerce Taiwan or to attempt an invasion. Taiwan's security rests on the PLA's difficulties in overcoming challenges to projecting power across the Taiwan Strait, the natural geographic advantages of island defense, the technological advantages and readiness of Taiwan's armed forces, and the possibility of US intervention to help defend Taiwan.

US security assistance, including but not limited to arms sales to Taiwan, is vital to deter China from coercing or attacking Taiwan, and to enable Taiwan's armed forces to fight effectively in all possible contingencies. The Obama administration has approved almost $14 billion in arms sales to Taiwan, which contribute to the island's ability to maintain a sufficient self-defense capability, provide moral support to the Taiwan people, and signal Beijing of US interest in Taiwan's security.

The existing process for considering and approving weapons for sale to Taiwan is not functioning well, however. Long delays in consulting with and notifying Congress and refusals to accept requests from Taiwan for advanced military equipment suggests a dysfunctional arrangement to the detriment of Taiwan's ability to maintain its ongoing force modernization. Moreover, in recent years, the US has been providing mostly second-hand equipment and additional munitions for systems already in Taiwan's inventory, while eschewing approval of new advanced platforms and weapons systems.

Worries that US-China relations, and Beijing's willingness to cooperate with the US in particular, will be undermined by the sale of more advanced capabilities to Taiwan, appear to be the root of the problem. Cooperation with China certainly presents important opportunities, for example to reverse global warming and prevent nuclear proliferation, and the US should seek to work with Beijing to address regional and global challenges where possible. However, it is harmful to American interests to be so eager for Chinese cooperation that it appears willing to sacrifice Taiwan for better US-China ties. Such an approach sends the wrong signal to Beijing, creates anxiety in Taiwan, and fosters doubt throughout the region about America's willingness to withstand Chinese pressure in support of its commitments.

A peaceful cross-Strait relationship is central to the stability and prosperity of the Asia-Pacific region and therefore is of vital importance to the United States. During the past 8 years under Ma Ying-jeou's rule, Beijing and Taipei have eased cross-Strait tensions and engaged in substantial, meaningful cooperation. The two sides established direct, scheduled flights between Taiwan and the Mainland, implemented direct shipping and postal services, signed 23 economic agreements, established a governmental channel and hotline between the Mainland's Taiwan Affairs Office and Taiwan's Mainland Affairs Council, and implemented additional measures to expand private, commercial and semi-official exchanges across the Strait. The improvement in cross-Strait relations culminated in a meeting between Taiwan's President Ma and Chinese President Xi Jinping in Singapore in November 2015. During the past 8 years, firm US support for Taiwan provided essential reassurance that helped Ma's administration engage in talks with Mainland China without fear of being bullied by Beijing or losing the confidence of Taiwan's citizens.

The election of Tsai Ing-wen, who will be inaugurated on May 20, has created some uncertainty about the future of the cross-Strait relationship. Both before and after the election, the Mainland has insisted that Tsai accept its definition of the "existing political foundation" of cross-Strait ties, which, for Beijing, includes opposition to Taiwan independence and the core of the "1992 Consensus"—that the two sides of the Strait belong to one China. Privately, Chinese officials have warned that unless Tsai accepts this definition, Beijing will suspend both the governmental and semi-governmental cross-Strait dialogue mechanisms. In addition, Mainland officials have hinted that they will drastically reduce the number of tourists from Mainland China to Taiwan, and may acquiesce to the requests of some of Taiwan's diplomatic allies to establish formal diplomatic ties with the PRC.

After her victory, Tsai Ing-wen, who throughout her campaign pledged that if elected she would maintain the cross-Strait status quo, provided additional reassurances to assuage Chinese fears about her intentions. In a January 21 interview with the Taiwan newspaper *Liberty Times*, Tsai stated that she "understands and respects" the historical fact that Taiwan and the Mainland held talks in 1992 and agreed to set aside their differences and seek common ground. She also maintained that the more than 20 years of exchanges and negotiations between the two sides of the Strait should be cherished and protected. In the interview, Tsai used the term "existing political foundation" of cross-Strait relations for the first time, offering her own definition that included the historical fact of the 1992 talks, the prevailing ROC constitutional order, the accumulated outcome of more than 20 years of cross-strait interaction, Taiwan's democratic principles and the will of the Taiwanese people.

Tsai appears to be making a sincere effort to find a new formulation that Taipei and Beijing can agree on, while insisting on their respective interpretations, so that cross-Strait stability and cooperation can be preserved. It remains to be seen whether this effort will be successful. In the remaining months before Tsai's inauguration, the US government can play a role to help narrow the gap between Mainland China and Taiwan by encouraging each side to provide assurances to the other to assuage their respective fears. The US should strongly discourage Beijing from using coercive measures to pressure Tsai and the DPP to concede to its demands. Punitive actions by China could compel Tsai Ing-wen to respond, perhaps by explicitly rejecting the "1992 Consensus," which so far she has carefully avoided. Beijing would interpret that as further proof that she cannot be trusted and the result would likely be a negative spiral that produces a cross-Strait setback or even a crisis. A US show of support, both from the Administration and Congress, for Tsai in the face of Beijing's pressures would be important to prevent a negative spiral.

Beijing appears to be deliberating how to respond to the DPP's return to power in Taiwan. The Mainland's annual Taiwan Affairs Work Conference, which convened in early February, encouraged promoting further cross-Strait economic integration, implementing steps to enhance the welfare of Taiwan compatriots, strengthening the protection of Taiwan businessmen's rights and interests, increasing people-to-people exchanges, and expanding exchanges with Taiwan parties and groups that uphold the one China principle. These recommendations are essentially an endorsement of the Mainland's current policy toward Taiwan, suggesting that Xi Jinping has not yet decided how to deal with Tsai Ing-wen.

With a host of issues already on his plate, including a slowing economy, the anti-corruption drive, and PLA reform, as well as challenges outside China's borders such as friction with neighbors in the East and South China Seas and North Korea's nuclear and missile tests, Xi would undoubtedly prefer to keep cross-Strait relations stable. On the other hand, Xi has demonstrated a tolerance for friction with a many of China's neighbors at the same time, and should Tsai press for *de jure* independence, he likely would not hesitate to take harsh economic, diplomatic and possibly even military measures.

Should Beijing lose confidence in its strategy of using economic integration to promote political reunification and conclude that its policy of promoting "peaceful development" across the Taiwan Strait has failed, it may opt for a more coercive, and even aggressive, approach toward Taiwan. If that occurs, the US response will be widely viewed as an indicator of the credibility of US commitments. Not only Japan, but also countries in Southeast Asia, would be alarmed if Washington failed to provide backing to Taiwan in the face of Chinese coercion or aggression.

For more than two decades, the US has insisted that decisions about Taiwan's future status must have the assent of the people of Taiwan in a democratic manner. Public opinion polls show that a majority of the Taiwan people favor talks with Mainland China, but dwindling numbers favor reunification. In 2015, a record-low 9.1 percent of respondents in the annual poll conducted since 1992 by National Chengchi University's Election Study Center favored unification either now or in the future, compared to 20 percent in 2003. In the same poll, 59.5 percent wanted to maintain the status quo for the time being or indefinitely, and 21.1 percent favored independence now or eventually.

Another National Chengchi University poll found that a record-low 3.3 percent of the Taiwan people regard themselves as Chinese and 59 percent identify themselves as Taiwanese. Those who said they consider themselves both Taiwanese and Chinese was 33.7 percent. The trend is evident: in 1992, 25.5 percent identified as Chinese, 17.6 percent identified as Taiwanese, and 46.4 percent identified as both Taiwanese and Chinese.

The polling data, combined with the outcome of the January 2016 election, suggests that a realignment of political forces and attitudes is underway in Taiwan. The landslide election of DPP candidate Tsai Ing-wen may signal more than the usual "throw the bums out" dynamic after 8 years of KMT rule. Rather, it may indicate that the people of Taiwan no longer support the KMT's approach to Mainland China, which has long included the goal of holding cross-Strait political talks and signing a peace treaty. Instead, they appear to favor economic interaction with mainland China, but not political integration. It is imperative that the US help Taiwan preserve the autonomy that its people desire and ensure that the differences between Taipei and Beijing be managed peacefully.

In addition to cross-Strait relations, a key security issue for the United States and other countries in the Asia-Pacific region is the South China Sea, where tensions have been rising in recent years. China's artificial island building and construction of facilities that can be used for military purposes, along with signals of intent to interfere with freedom of navigation, have been the main source of these tensions. Beijing's ambiguous territorial claims and its refusal to clarify them publicly have raised concerns throughout the region that it will ultimately seek to control the area inside the nine-dashed line, a map of which China submitted to the UN in May 2009. In the accompanying *Note Verbale*, China referenced the nine-dashed line map, stating that it "has indisputable sovereignty over the islands in the South China Sea, and the adjacent waters, and enjoys sovereign rights and jurisdiction over the relevant waters as well as the seabed and subsoil thereof."

The Philippines filed a case at the International Tribunal for the Law of the Sea (ITLOS) in January 2013 seeking to invalidate China's nine-dashed line, among other charges. In October 2015, the Tribunal ruled that under the United Nations Convention on the Law of the Sea (UNCLOS) it has jurisdiction on seven of the submissions raised by the Philippines. A hearing on the merits of the case was held in late November. The Tribunal will likely issue a ruling in mid-2016 and most legal experts believe there is a strong possibility that it will find that the nine-dashed line has no basis in international law. Although any decision of the Tribunal will be legally binding on both the Philippines and China, Beijing has already stated that it rejects the jurisdiction of the tribunal and that its rulings will have no binding effect on China.

Taiwan's role in this dispute is important because China's nine-dashed line claim derives from an eleven-dashed line drawn on a map that the Republic China released in 1947. Like Beijing, Taipei has been ambiguous about the meaning of its map and the extent of its claim. Despite appeals from the United States to clarify the intent behind the 1947 map by fully opening its archives to public scrutiny, the KMT has refused to do so. Moreover, Ma Ying-jeou's administration rejected the award issued by the Tribunal on the jurisdictional question, stating that since the ROC was not invited to participate in the arbitration, "the ROC neither recognizes nor accepts related awards."

If, as evidence so far suggests, the archives in Taiwan reveal that the ROC government intended to lay claim only to the land features inside the eleven-dashed line, but not the waters, this would de-legitimize Beijing's claim and put pressure on China to bring its claim into conformity with international law, especially UNCLOS. Combined with a possible ruling against China by the UNCLOS Tribunal, Taipei's action could aid in changing Beijing's calculus and its overall approach to the South China Sea. In addition, by being transparent about the original ROC 1947 claim, Taiwan can remind the other claimants and the international community that it has important interests at stake in the South China Sea and signal that it is willing to be a constructive player in managing the dispute.

The DPP has so far adopted a nuanced and cautious approach to the South China Sea. In various statements, the DPP has called for all parties to assert their claims and positions in accordance with UNCLOS, maintain freedom of navigation and flight in the area, and work to resolve their disputes peacefully. I believe that the new government, once it takes power, will try to strike a prudent balance between avoiding a confrontation with Beijing on the South China Sea and being a transparent, law abiding, responsible member of the international community.

Preserving cross-Strait peace and stability is a very high priority for the United States, and an early action by Tsai Ing-wen's administration on the South China Sea that riles Beijing could feed Chinese suspicions of the DPP and thus undermine stability. Therefore, the timing of a decision by Taiwan to open its archives, should it choose to do so, must be carefully considered. The South China Sea should not become the catalyst of a downward spiral in relations between Taipei and Beijing. The DPP's response to the pending award by the Tribunal later this year, must also be weighed carefully.

Nevertheless, Taiwan potentially has a unique role to play in the global effort to persuade Mainland China to abide by a rules-based order and rely on diplomacy to resolve the territorial disputes in the South China Sea. The US should be in close consultation with President-elect Tsai during the coming months and after the inauguration on the South China Sea as well as many on other issues.

A robust bilateral US-Taiwan relationship is essential to American interests today and in the future. The role of Congress in strengthening US-Taiwan relations remains indispensable and there are many actions that Congress can take in addition to holding this hearing to further advance the bilateral relationship as well as Taiwan's prosperity and security. I urge Congress to invigorate its oversight role and to encourage the executive branch to be more ambitious in promoting closer US-Taiwan relations.

Members of Congress should travel more frequently to Taiwan to better understand the evolving political and economic situation. Exchanges with Taiwan's

Legislative Yuan should be expanded with a focus on advising LY members on how to better use professional staff, establish staffed committees, and perform a more effective oversight role. Congress can also devote more attention to educating its members and constituents about why Taiwan is important to American interests. Congress can continue to urge the executive branch to develop strategies to further develop Taiwan's meaningful participation in the US-affiliated bodies and other multilateral organizations. Finally, Congress can encourage the administration to sell Taiwan the weapons necessary for it to deter a PRC attack and defend itself from PRC aggression.

Mr. SALMON. Dr. Rigger.

STATEMENT OF SHELLEY RIGGER, PH.D., BROWN PROFESSOR AND ASSISTANT DEAN FOR EDUCATIONAL POLICY, DAVIDSON COLLEGE

Ms. RIGGER. Thank you very much for allowing me to be here. It's a pleasure to have this opportunity.

Taiwan's January elections were a watershed in the island's democratic development. For the first time, the Kuomintang lost control of both branches of the national government.

The DPP has won national elections only twice before when Chen Shui-bian was elected President in 2000 and 2004, and many in Washington remember the Chen presidency as a time of turbulence.

Chen began his presidency with efforts to reach out to Beijing and to the KMT but both the PRC and the KMT stonewalled and he eventually gave up on seeking their cooperation and began pursuing an agenda aimed more at pleasing his core supporters.

Nonetheless, the Chen presidency left many voters feeling disillusioned and that helped give the KMT's Ma Ying-jeou an easy win in 2008.

Under Ma, the Taiwan Strait has been relatively calm. Taiwan has signed almost two dozen economic agreements with the PRC while cross-Strait trade, investment and people to people flows have increased to unprecedented levels.

So now that the DPP is about to return to power, people are asking whether we are about to enter another era of tension in the Taiwan Strait.

While I understand why these questions are being asked, I do not believe we are about to enter an era of confrontation. Under Tsai's leadership, the DPP has adopted moderate positions that align with the preferences of Taiwan's people.

Throughout her campaign she made it clear that her goal is to preserve the status quo in the Taiwan Strait. She does not intend to move Taiwan toward independence but neither does she intend to rush headlong into Beijing's embrace, either politically or economically.

So, in short, the January elections affirmed Taiwan's democracy and confirmed the fundamental rationality of Taiwan's electorate.

Promoting democracy is a core interest and objective of U.S. foreign policy. During the Cold War, Taiwan's Government persuaded the U.S. to overlook its authoritarian nature but in the '70s and '80s U.S. officials, especially Members of Congress, joined with democracy activists in Taiwan to urge the KMT-led government to implement democratic reforms. Taiwan's democratization was achieved with almost no bloodshed or instability, making it an example to other nations.

Supporting Taiwan's democracy is an important element of U.S. policy, therefore, and it is critical that we not confuse Taiwan's people's active defense of their democracy with trouble making.

An overwhelming majority of Taiwanese recognize that pursuing formal independence is both unnecessary and risky but they have no interest in being absorbed into the People's Republic of China.

Their goal is to remain a self-governing democratic entity while working toward peaceful and cooperative relations with their neighbors on the Chinese mainland.

These goals, which are represented well now that Tsai has been elected the U.S. should redouble its efforts to keep channels of communication open.

U.S. policy precludes Washington from engaging in high-level official interactions with Taipei, although it seems that not everyone in this room thinks that's a good policy.

But the U.S. is free to choose a less restrictive interpretation of its policy. Overly rigid adherence to the one-China policy will not serve the U.S. well in a period of uncertainty and transition.

The task for the U.S. in the next few years will be to support Taiwan's continued democratic development. Washington should recognize and reward the DPP-led government's moderate positions and encourage all parties to seek opportunities for cooperation and avoid confrontation.

Given Taipei and Beijing's incompatible goals in some areas, a degree of tension is unavoidable. However, attentive management can prevent that tension from ripening into conflict.

Thank you very much.

[The prepared statement of Ms. Rigger follows:]

Testimony for the Hearing on the Future of U.S.-Taiwan Relations
Subcommittee on Asia and the Pacific, Committee on Foreign Affairs

Shelley Rigger, Davidson College

Taiwan's January 16, 2016 elections were an important watershed in the island's democratic development. For the first time, the Kuomintang (KMT, or Nationalist Party), lost control of both branches of the national government when its long-time opponent, the Democratic Progressive Party (DPP), won the presidency and 68 out of 113 legislative seats.

The DPP has won national elections only twice before. In 2000, the DPP candidate Chen Shui-bian was elected president in a three-way race, but the KMT and its allies retained a legislative majority throughout presidency, including after his reelection in 2004.

Many in Washington remember the Chen presidency as a time of turbulence in cross-Strait relations and in U.S.-Taiwan relations. Chen began his presidency with efforts to reach out to Beijing and to his KMT opponents: his inaugural address included "Five Noes" aimed at calming the PRC's fears that he might try to make Taiwan formally independent, and he appointed a KMT politician as his first premier. Nonetheless, the PRC and the KMT both stonewalled Chen, and he eventually gave up on seeking their cooperation and began pursuing an agenda aimed at pleasing his core supporters. In 2003 he initiated two projects – creating a referendum mechanism and campaigning for a new constitution – which many policymakers in Beijing and Washington viewed as thinly-disguised moves toward Taiwan independence. Neither project succeeded as Chen had hoped.

In his first term Chen found himself stymied by resistance from the KMT-dominated legislature. That resistance continued in his second term, while a series of scandals added to Chen's troubles. The Chen presidency left many voters feeling disillusioned and frustrated, which helped give the KMT's presidential candidate Ma Ying-jeou an easy win in 2008. For the eight years Ma was in office the Taiwan Strait was relatively calm. Under Ma, Taiwan signed almost two dozen economic agreements with the PRC, while cross-Strait trade, investment, and people-to-people flows increased to unprecedented levels.

Now that the DPP is about to return to power – and without a KMT legislative majority to check it – questions are arising as to whether we are about to enter another era of tension in the Taiwan Strait. Will the new president, Tsai Ying-wen, take after Chen, her predecessor? Will the DPP, emboldened by its landslide victories and legislative majority, attempt to realize its long-dormant ambition for formal independence? If so, how should the U.S. respond?

While I understand why these questions are being asked, I do not believe we are about to enter an era of confrontation. If we do find ourselves in such an era, it will not be because Tsai Ying-wen and her party recklessly pursued dangerous goals. Under Tsai's leadership, the DPP has adopted moderate positions that align with the preferences of Taiwan's people. While dissatisfaction with the previous president and disarray within the KMT were important factors driving the January election results, the DPP would not have had the victories it did had it not met the voters' expectations and presented policies in line with their preferences. In short, the

January 2016 elections affirmed Taiwan's democracy and confirmed the fundamental rationality of Taiwan's electorate.

Over the past eight years, even as relations with mainland China grew closer, Taiwan's domestic economy faltered. The Ma Administration assured islanders that the solution to their economic woes was even tighter cross-Strait economic cooperation, tailored to the interests of large companies doing business in the mainland. Ma's assurances have fallen on increasingly deaf ears in the past few years, as more and more Taiwanese have begun to question whether the route to widely-shared prosperity really does pass through mainland China. Tsai Ying-wen offered an alternative view, that Taiwan should be more wary in its relations with the mainland, and should focus its policies on developing the island's domestic economy, reducing inequality, and diversifying its economic partners. This is a moderate position, one that reflects Taiwan voters' growing hesitancy regarding cross-Strait engagement.

Throughout her campaign, Dr. Tsai made it clear that her goal is to preserve the status quo in the Taiwan Strait. In other words, she does not intend to move Taiwan toward independence, but neither does she intend to rush headlong into Beijing's embrace, either economic or political. Here again, her positions align with those of the electorate.

President Ma shares Dr. Tsai's commitment to preserving the status quo. Neither politician believes Taiwan should agree to China's demand for unification. Where the two differ is on the strategies they favor for achieving their common objective. Ma was willing to work within a framework tacitly worked out in 1992 – known as the '92 Consensus – under which Taipei and Beijing agree that both Taiwan and the mainland are part of a single Chinese nation, the precise interpretation of which differs on the two sides. The PRC leadership emphasizes the "One China" element of the '92 Consensus, while Taiwan's leaders have emphasized the "different interpretations" element. The '92 Consensus is a thin reed on which to base this important relationship, but it has been strong enough to enable cross-Strait talks during periods of KMT government (it was dormant during the Chen Administration).

Tsai Ying-wen has so far declined to accept the '92 Consensus as the basis for cross-Strait talks. Her party has long rejected the characterization of the agreement as a "consensus;" DPP leaders maintain that the label was created after the fact and does not accurately described what happened in 1992. Meanwhile, Beijing's eagerness to repackage Taiwan's acceptance of the formula as acquiescence to its "One China Principle" (the idea that Taiwan is part of the PRC) makes it extremely hard for Tsai to accept it. Still, Tsai has said that she would like to move cross-Strait relations forward on the basis of the accumulated outcomes of 20-plus years of cross-Strait interactions – a statement DPP officials say is intended to recognize the utility of the '92 Consensus, if not its label.

When Tsai first stood for election in the 2012 presidential race, her inability to articulate a clear position on the '92 Consensus undermined the confidence of many Taiwanese voters as well as U.S. officials. At that time, many in both groups believed accepting the '92 Consensus was necessary for a potential president to successfully manage cross-Strait relations, which Taiwan's voters, in particular, viewed as a prerequisite for Taiwan's continued prosperity. This year, both parts of that statement were less persuasive, and Tsai's refusal to endorse the '92 Consensus no longer worked against her politically. Meanwhile, Tsai's more careful rhetoric in 2016, which she unfolded in a speech at CSIS in Washington last June, satisfied officials in Washington that her cross-Strait policies would be guided by prudence and flexibility rather than ideological purism.

Another reason for the DPP's success in January's elections was the KMT's poor political performance over the past three years. The KMT has bungled important challenges, and it has been riven by disastrous internal conflicts. The election results were a clear message to the KMT: it needs to pull itself together and present a coherent, attractive program and unified leadership. For the KMT to make such a recovery is important for Taiwan's continued democratic thriving.

Promoting democracy is a core interest and objective of U.S. foreign policy. The U.S. has long supported emerging democracies around the world, but Taiwan's democracy is a particularly valuable example. As a "bulwark against communist expansion" during the Cold War, Taiwan's government persuaded the U.S. to overlook its authoritarian nature, but in the 1970s and '80s, U.S. officials – especially Members of Congress – joined with democracy activists in Taiwan to urge the KMT-led government to implement democratic reform. Taiwan's democratization was achieved with almost no bloodshed or instability, making it an example to other nations hoping to follow a similar course.

Supporting and protecting Taiwan's maturing democracy is an important element of U.S. policy, and it is critical that we not confuse Taiwan people's active defense of that democracy for "troublemaking." An overwhelming majority of Taiwanese recognize that pursuing formal independence is both unnecessary and risky, but they have no interest in being absorbed into the People's Republic of China. Their goal is to remain a self-governing, democratic entity while working toward peaceful and cooperative relations with their neighbors on the Chinese mainland. Their goals – which are represented well in Tsai Ying-wen's platform – pose no threat to the U.S. or any other nation.

It is likely that there will be some tension in the Taiwan Strait during Tsai's term of office, but I do not expect it will result from provocation by Taiwan. Rather, tension is the inevitable result of the profound difference in goals between Taiwan and mainland China. As long as Beijing insists that Taiwan must accept unification, no matter which party governs in Taipei there will be tension, because Beijing's demands run against the will of Taiwan's people.

America's interests are served when cross-Strait relations are peaceful and stable; both sides should be encouraged to engage with one another in ways that promote peace and stability. Taiwan is managing its relationship with the mainland in a way that allows the two sides to cooperate on many things while avoiding political unification. It is when leaders try to force outcomes that violate popular will that confrontation arises. If, despite efforts to dissuade them, PRC leaders decide to freeze out Tsai as they did Chen Shui-bian, the U.S. government should resist Beijing's efforts to label Taiwan as the guilty party.

A strength of U.S. policy in recent years is the Obama Administration's efforts to improve communication and understanding between the U.S. government and the Democratic Progressive Party. These efforts, which have included meetings with DPP officials in Washington as well as on-going communications through the American Institute in Taiwan (AIT), the U.S.'s de facto embassy in Taipei, have helped to reduce uncertainty and increase American officials' confidence that the Tsai Administration will avoid the kind of negative surprises that soured relations between the U.S. and the Chen Administration. Now that Tsai has been elected, the U.S. should redouble its efforts to keep those channels of communication open. U.S. policy precludes Washington from engaging in high-level, official interactions with Taipei, but the U.S. is free to choose a less restrictive interpretation of its policy. Overly-rigid adherence to the One China Policy will not serve the U.S. well in a period of uncertainty and transition.

The task for the U.S. in the next few years will be to support and encourage Taiwan's continued democratic development and strong economic contribution. Washington should also recognize and reward the DPP-led government's moderate positions. Finally, the U.S. government should encourage all parties in the region to seek opportunities for cooperation and avoid unnecessary confrontation. Given Taipei and Beijing's incompatible goals in some areas, a degree of tension is unavoidable. However, attentive management can prevent that tension from ripening into confrontation, while allowing the two sides to cooperate in those arenas in which their goals are not incompatible.

Witness's Biography

Shelley Rigger is the Brown Professor of East Asian Politics, Chair of Chinese Studies and Assistant Dean for Educational Policy at Davidson College. She has a PhD in Government from Harvard University and a BA in Public and International Affairs from Princeton University. She has been a visiting researcher at National Chengchi University in Taiwan (2005) and a visiting professor at Fudan University (2006) and Shanghai Jiaotong University (2013 & 2015). She is a non-resident fellow of the China Policy Institute at Nottingham University and a senior fellow of the Foreign Policy Research Institute (FPRI). Rigger is the author of two books on Taiwan's domestic politics, *Politics in Taiwan: Voting for Democracy* (Routledge 1999) and *From Opposition to Power: Taiwan's Democratic Progressive Party* (Lynne Rienner Publishers 2001). In 2011 she published *Why Taiwan Matters: Small Island, Global Powerhouse,* a book for general readers. She has published articles on Taiwan's domestic politics, the national identity issue in Taiwan-China relations and related topics. Her monograph, "Taiwan's Rising Rationalism: Generations, Politics and 'Taiwan Nationalism'" was published by the East West Center in Washington in November 2006. Currently she is working on a study of Taiwan's contributions to the PRC's economic take-off.

Mr. SALMON. Thank you.

When I first came to Congress in the '90s, Warren Christopher was the Secretary of State and I remember him coming before one of our committees and testifying that our policy with China and Taiwan was one of strategic ambiguity.

I thought that was the stupidest thing I'd ever heard in my life, and my understanding is that's still our policy. Is it or isn't it? Dr. Rigger, do you want to take a stab at that?

Ms. RIGGER. Sure. Yes, it is our policy and the—I think part of the reason it continues to be our policy is that it has—whatever its merits on the face of it actually served us very well for a long time.

So it might not be the policy that a political scientist would design but I don't recommend government by a political scientist. So I think in practice it has allowed the U.S. to calibrate its actions and positions toward both the PRC and Taiwan in ways that have successfully maintained the balance in the Strait.

Mr. SALMON. But what it's yielded is really idiotic policies like when Lee Teng-hui couldn't visit his alma mater at Cornell and we had to pass special legislation encouraging or allowing him to do so.

Or Taiwan virtually being kicked out of every international body and now we have to try to assert in the name of common sense that they be allowed to participate in bodies like Interpol when we're all—we want all hands on deck to fight international terrorism and international crime and trafficking—in human trafficking.

It just makes sense to have all hands on deck. And why in the world would anybody in Taiwan ever want to follow up on China's offer of peaceful reunification with a one-China two systems when they see how they hoodwink the people of Hong Kong?

Universal suffrage—you know, the folks in Hong Kong believe that claptrap that Beijing was throwing at them that, you know, it's going to be one-China, two systems when in reality the leader of Hong Kong gets picked by Beijing. Why would Taiwan ever want to yield to that?

Ms. Glaser, do you have any thoughts?

Ms. GLASER. Well, I think that that's exactly the reason why the polls show that the people of Taiwan—very few of them actually support reunification as they observe Hong Kong, as they witness the crackdown on dissent and the squeezing of the ability of average people on the mainland just to access Internet, to conduct protests, to publish their views.

I think it's clear that people in Taiwan do not want to be part of the mainland and do not support one country, two systems.

Mr. SALMON. Oh, and in Taiwan proselytizing is legal. People can share their religious views freely. They have freedom of the press.

You have peaceful transitions from one, you know, party to the next in leadership and the President's office and in the seat of government, and they see the vast differences when you speak about your—with conviction.

I guess you can believe in something as long as you don't really believe it in China and that's—you know, that's the problem. If you really believe in something then you're a fanatic and you get imprisoned.

And so, you know, the people of Taiwan watch this stuff happening and they're very cautious. Look, I was as concerned as anybody with some of the statements that Chen Shui-bian was making, you know, later on in his administration.

But Tsai Ing-wen has said that she intends to promote the status quo. She's not trying to upset the apple cart but she's made it clear that her first interest and first duty is to the people of Taiwan, not to the people on mainland China. I don't think that's all that extreme. I think that's just common sense.

And so as they go forward, how can we monitor, you know, in our relations with the cross-Strait? What indicators should we be monitoring for a sense of how the cross-Strait relationship is being handled between China and the DPP, whether or not they're going to stonewall her like they did Chen Shui-bian?

I guess that's one thing we could probably see pretty readily. But the other one is what do you expect will happen to current formal official contact between the two sides of the Strait? Do you think there's going to be any degradation of that?

Ms. GLASER. Thank you, Congressman Salmon.

I think those are very important questions. As to indicators, one of the early indicators we can look at is whether the mainland is restricting tourists that are travelling to Taiwan. There are already some signs of that. This could damage Taiwan's economy and the mainland, of course, claims some deniability. They say oh, maybe the people of mainland just don't want to go. But we know that this is in fact government control.

I particularly worry about the possibility of Beijing trying to steal away some of Taiwan's diplomatic allies. Taiwan now has 22 and there are some countries who have indicated a desire to shift their diplomatic allegiance.

So far Beijing has respected this tacit diplomatic truce. But I think that this could put pressure on President Tsai once she is inaugurated to respond in a negative way that could lead to that downward sort of negative spiral that I talked about.

As for the formal communications, I think that so far Beijing has not said publically that they are going to cut those off but privately there are some indications that the semi-official white glove organizations, SEF and ARATS on both sides of the Strait could be suspended and also the communications between the Taiwan affairs office and the mainland affairs council where they recently set up a hotline and those could also be suspended. I think any suspension of communication and dialogue channels would be a very negative sign.

Mr. SALMON. I'm just going to close with this and then yield to Mr. Sherman. But, you know, a position of strategic ambiguity would be when a Member of Congress asks the panelist, you know, how do you feel about Taiwan participation in the second round of the TPP and the answer coming back, we welcome their interest in that, that's a position of strategic ambiguity out there in the ozone.

A strategic clarity statement would be yes, we welcome their involvement, their participation—not their interest. But we—like you said, Mr. Schriver, would you agree with that?

Mr. SCHRIVER. Absolutely, and I think that a lot has changed since Warren Christopher was secretary of state and I think the very positive developments on Taiwan should be recognized and rewarded but also the threat posture that China poses I think would be served with more clarity when it comes to defense commitments and security in a whole host of areas including these trade agreements and international organizations.

I think ambiguity maybe had its time and place but more clarity is probably appropriate at this juncture.

Mr. SALMON. Yes, let's just stop parsing words and say what we mean.

Mr. Sherman.

Mr. SHERMAN. I'll make a couple of political science comments.

First, in defense of strategic ambiguity, Donald Trump is not known for has ambiguity yet he has spoken often in favor of not saying what he would do because that gives—would give him—a Trump presidency—more leverage in the negotiations.

The problem with it I find with strategic ambiguity is that it means that if you're going to keep the foreign power guessing as to what our policy is then you cannot inform the American people of what.

So I think if we had a dictatorship there would be—in the United States it would fit with strategic ambiguity and I don't know if that's what Mr. Trump has in mind but he doesn't talk to me.

Mr. SALMON. He doesn't talk to me either.

Mr. SHERMAN. Also, the second political science comment is political scientists live in this world where you figure out what is the interest of the country as if this was a game of Risk or something where the country was a single entity determining its interests.

My own belief is that countries make foreign policy decisions to respond to short-term domestic political needs, and right now China needs nationalism to explain why a party that is no longer the vanguard of the proletariat should continue to rule in the absence of 7½ percent growth.

Dr. Rigger, what—putting pressure on Taiwan, is that popular with Joe Six-pack in Shanghai?

Ms. RIGGER. It's extremely difficult for us to know what is popular with the citizens of the People's Republic of China because it is not an open information environment.

What is more troubling even than that though is that there is a certain kind of Joe Six-pack in the mainland who is allowed to speak and is allowed to speak loudly and perpetually.

Mr. SHERMAN. Well, we know that nationalism over the islets or rocks or whatever we're going to fight World War III about in the South Pacific that's popular nationalism. Is it consistent with popular nationalism in China to say we're going to be tough on Taiwan or—I mean, you're being tough on Chinese people.

So is a—does it fit with jingoistic popular nationalism in China to try to kick Taiwan out of Interpol?

Ms. RIGGER. It does. But it's hard for—it's impossible to understand what that really means in terms of China's long-term domestic political situation because——

Mr. SHERMAN. You need to study political science by running for office. There are no long-term political objectives. There are short-term political objectives.

Ms. RIGGER. Can I explain though what my logic is? So the problem is that in China there are few things that you can say out loud and all of them are I hate Japan, we should be more aggressive in the South China Sea, Taiwan must be reunified with the mainland.

But we don't know whether people would be saying those things as loudly and energetically as they are if they could say other things.

Mr. SHERMAN. Okay.

Ms. RIGGER. But because they can't say other things, these are the things they say.

Mr. SHERMAN. What—okay. Ms. Glaser talked a little bit about the things China can do to show its displeasure with the fact that the Taiwanese people voted for what they consider to be the wrong political party.

Those all seem like little nitpicking. Is there anything China might do to Taiwan in the next year that is more significant than trying to get a Latin American country to cut off diplomatic relations or giving Taiwan the cold shoulder and stopping communication with various mainland entities? Anything——

Ms. RIGGER. Within the next year, probably not. But those small things, especially added together, can have a really profound effect on the confidence of Taiwan people and their ability to go forward strongly and to advocate for their own interests. So they do matter.

Mr. SHERMAN. If five Embassies closed in Taipei from countries that many Taiwanese could not find on a map would that shake confidence?

Ms. RIGGER. Yes, and if ten closed that would be half of Taiwan's diplomatic partners in the world.

Mr. SHERMAN. Well, that's why I asked about five.

Ms. RIGGER. And that would deeply shake people's confidence, absolutely.

Mr. SHERMAN. Ah, there are a few islands that are so small that they would appreciate even modest aid from Taiwan. New Embassies could be opened by countries that are even harder to find on a map.

Okay. What factors do you believe contributed to the DPP winning the elections and, just as significantly, the KMT's weak showing?

Ms. RIGGER. I think the biggest issues were domestic issues for Taiwan. Economic issues—the sense that Taiwan's economy can produce aggregate growth at a slow but reasonable rate but that it can't produce jobs or the kinds of jobs that Taiwanese people are preparing themselves to do as they emerge from school and it can't produce the kind of egalitarian distribution of income and wealth that Taiwanese have come to expect as the fruit of development.

Mr. SHERMAN. Sounds like Bernie Sanders won the election.

Ms. RIGGER. Well, I think that the problems that Taiwan faces are not Taiwan's alone.

Mr. SHERMAN. Okay. And what can the DPP Government and Taiwan in general do to lessen its dependence on mainland China?

Ms. RIGGER. This is the great task facing Taiwan to figure out the answer to this question. The DPP has published lots of white papers and statements about what they plan to do. But most of those are pretty vague and piecemeal.

The best thing that Taiwan could do, I think, is to improve its accessibility to international trade and investment. Taiwan still has a lot of parts of its market and economy that are not very open and I think that's really what we are talking about when we talk about getting ready for TPP.

The international business community has been asking a long time for Taiwan to open its economy more and I think perhaps Taiwan can make some progress there.

Mr. SHERMAN. I have gone over time. I don't know if the other witnesses have any quick comments.

Ms. GLASER. I would just make one quick comment and that is that the mainland China has a pretty robust toolbox to use to pressure Taiwan.

There's economic tools, there's preferences that they give to Taiwan businesses on the mainland, there's fish that they buy from southern Taiwan fisherman.

They can cut all of these. Only two countries have been really permitted, and I put that in quotation marks, to negotiate bilateral free trade averments with Taiwan.

That's Singapore and New Zealand, and there are other countries that had started informal talks, those who want to begin talks, and Beijing has basically shut that down.

They have diplomatic economic influence directly on Taiwan and then indirectly through other countries so—and then, of course, there's the whole toolbox of military coercion. So I think there's a lot to be concerned about.

Mr. SCHRIVER. Briefly on that last point, we shouldn't forget about the military piece of this because throughout this 8-year period of peace and stability what has China done on the military side?

They have continued to build up more missiles, more capabilities, more training. They have a mock-up of the presidential palace that they're exercising against. I mean, countries that equip, train, prepare——

Mr. SHERMAN. They have a mock-up of Taiwan's presidential palace so they can train special forces into how to go in and seize the President or something like that?

Mr. SCHRIVER. Yes, sir.

Mr. SHERMAN. Oh. I might point out, if we really cared about Taiwan's defense we would just amend the law that provided most favoured nation status to China and say this law is void if China takes military action against Taiwan, its ports and its shipping.

And some of us tried to do that back when we first gave affirmative MFN—that it's not too late. That one—they wouldn't need the frigates if we did that.

Mr. SALMON. I thank the panel. This has been very, very, very helpful. Thank you very much.

One just last question. You had mentioned that there were four things and I think we got three. Would the fourth be Tibet?

I mean, are they still—because every time I ever met with senior Beijing officials the two things that, you know, was like drilling on their teeth without novocaine was Taiwan Strait and Tibet. Is that still pretty much the same thing.

Ms. RIGGER. You can say anything you want to about those issues and not get in trouble. So if you want to speak out on those topics, it's fine.

Mr. SALMON. Right. Right.

Well, thank you very much. I really appreciate the panel and thank the ranking member. It's been very edifying and I want to congratulate the people of Taiwan again on a wonderfully successful and peaceful election and transition that's about to happen and also let them know that we're with you in spirit and in every other way in relationship to rebuilding after the earthquake.

So thank you very much.

Mr. SHERMAN. I agree.

Mr. SALMON. This committee is adjourned.

[Whereupon, at 4:15 p.m., the subcommittee was adjourned.]

APPENDIX

MATERIAL SUBMITTED FOR THE RECORD

SUBCOMMITTEE HEARING NOTICE
COMMITTEE ON FOREIGN AFFAIRS
U.S. HOUSE OF REPRESENTATIVES
WASHINGTON, DC 20515-6128

Subcommittee on Asia and the Pacific
Matt Salmon (R-AZ), Chairman

February 9, 2016

TO: MEMBERS OF THE COMMITTEE ON FOREIGN AFFAIRS

You are respectfully requested to attend an OPEN hearing of the Committee on Foreign Affairs, to be held by the Subcommittee on Asia and the Pacific in Room 2200 of the Rayburn House Office Building (and available live on the Committee website at http://www.ForeignAffairs.house.gov):

DATE: Thursday, February 11, 2016

TIME: 2:00 p.m.

SUBJECT: The Future of U.S.-Taiwan Relations

WITNESSES: Panel I
                   Ms. Susan A. Thornton
                   Deputy Assistant Secretary
                   Bureau of East Asian and Pacific Affairs
                   U.S. Department of State

                   Panel II
                   Mr. Randall Schriver
                   President and Chief Executive Officer
                   Project 2049 Institute

                   Ms. Bonnie Glaser
                   Senior Adviser for Asia
                   Director of China Power Project
                   Center for Strategic and International Studies

                   Shelley Rigger, Ph.D.
                   Brown Professor and Assistant Dean for Educational Policy
                   Davidson College

**NOTE: Further witnesses may be added.

By Direction of the Chairman

The Committee on Foreign Affairs seeks to make its facilities accessible to persons with disabilities. If you are in need of special accommodations, please call 202/225-5021 at least four business days in advance of the event, whenever practicable. Questions with regard to special accommodations in general (including availability of Committee materials in alternative formats and assistive listening devices) may be directed to the Committee.

COMMITTEE ON FOREIGN AFFAIRS

MINUTES OF SUBCOMMITTEE ON _____Asia and the Pacific_____ HEARING

Day___*Thursday*___Date___*February 11th, 2016*___Room_____*2200*_____

Starting Time ____*2:00pm*____Ending Time ____*4:15pm*____

Recesses |__-__| (____to____) (____to____) (____to____) (____to____) (____to____) (____to____)

Presiding Member(s)

Matt Salmon

Check all of the following that apply:

Open Session ☑   Electronically Recorded (taped) ☐
Executive (closed) Session ☐   Stenographic Record ☐
Televised ☐

TITLE OF HEARING:

The Future of U.S.-Taiwan Relations

SUBCOMMITTEE MEMBERS PRESENT:

Dana Rohrabacher, Steve Chabot
Brad Sherman, Ami Bera, Alan Lowenthal, Gerald Connolly, Grace Meng

---

NON-SUBCOMMITTEE MEMBERS PRESENT: *(Mark with an * if they are not members of full committee.)*

Ed Royce

HEARING WITNESSES: Same as meeting notice attached? Yes ☑ No ☐
(If "no", please list below and include title, agency, department, or organization.)

-

STATEMENTS FOR THE RECORD: *(List any statements submitted for the record.)*

Gerald Connolly

TIME SCHEDULED TO RECONVENE ____-____
or
TIME ADJOURNED ____*4:15pm*____

_____
Subcommittee Staff Director

Statement for the Record
Submitted by Mr. Connolly of Virginia

The U.S. and Taiwan have developed a dynamic relationship based on our shared values, deep economic ties, and a history of bilateral collaboration. The U.S. commitment to Taiwan is a sacred obligation, and it should not be cheapened by characterizing the relationship as a way to rebuke China. U.S.-Taiwan relations are important in their own right.

Secretary of State John Kerry testified before the House Committee on Foreign Affairs last year on the FY2016 Foreign Affairs Budget. In response to a question I submitted during that hearing regarding Taiwan's role in the rebalance to the Asia-Pacific, Secretary Kerry stated, "Taiwan is a key component of U.S. Asia-Pacific policies, including the Asia rebalance. The United States continues to expand and enhance its strong and multifaceted unofficial relationship with Taiwan. Taiwan is an important security and economic partner of the United States, an important part of global value chains, a vibrant democracy, and our tenth-largest trading partner."

He went on to cite the Trade and Investment Framework Agreement process, Taiwan's future accession to the Trans-Pacific Partnership, and the provision of defense articles and services to Taiwan as ways in which the U.S. will demonstrate continued commitment to Taiwan.

From the perspective of a co-Chair of the Congressional Taiwan Caucus, this is a welcome statement from Secretary Kerry that faithfully upholds our existing obligations to Taiwan, and it is consistent with what should be a guiding principle of the rebalance – demonstrated resolve to support our existing partners in the region.

The U.S. has a longstanding commitment to Taiwan and its defensive capability that should be fully upheld in the interest of resolving cross-strait disputes. This obligation was enshrined into law with the enactment of the Taiwan Relations Act in April 1979. In the TRA, the U.S. committed to resisting the use of coercion to determine the future of Taiwan and to provide Taiwan with the necessary defense articles "to maintain a sufficient self-defense capability."

In early December, the House Committee on Foreign Affairs reported out the Taiwan Naval Support Act (H.R. 4154), which called on the Administration to develop and report a timeframe for naval vessel transfers authorized by the Naval Vessel Transfer Act of 2013 (Public Law 113–276). Later that month, the Administration made the welcome announcement that it had authorized a $1.83 billion arms sales package for Taiwan that included two frigates and other defense articles.

I look forward to hearing from our witnesses today regarding ways in which the U.S. will continue to support the tenets of the TRA and further develop this important relationship.

We should be encouraged by the recent elections held in Taiwan which were – by all accounts – free, fair, and open elections. The U.S. should help facilitate a peaceful transfer of power – the hallmark of a mature democracy – and work with President-elect Tsai Ing-wen to define common priorities and identify the next frontier of U.S.-Taiwan relations.

We should recognize that Taiwan's position in the world is fraught with challenges. The recent attacks on democracy in Hong Kong are not reassuring to any democratic system in the Asia-Pacific, and tensions in the South China Sea are a proximate regional flashpoint. However, Taiwan has proven itself to be a resilient partner – going from aid recipient in the 1950s and 1960s to becoming our 10th largest trading partner. There are more complicated and contentious issues of trade liberalization on the horizon, but U.S.-Taiwan relations are worthy of ambitious goals and energetic collaboration.